Prepare Your Heart

A 40-Day Lenten Devotional Using Anglican Prayer Beads to Prepare Your Heart for Easter

Kathryn Shirey

Introduction

Welcome! I'm so glad you've decided to take up this devotional for Lent and I pray it will be a moving, Holy Lenten season for you.

I was initially asked to write this devotional by one of the ministry directors at my church. They wanted a Lenten devotional for the congregation, but also wanted to introduce prayer beads as a form of prayer. She had DIY kits to hand out at the Shrove Tuesday dinner to make your Anglican prayer beads and wanted a prayer guide to accompany them for Lent.

I honestly had been hesitant to explore prayer beads. This wasn't the first request I'd had to write about praying with prayer beads, but I still wasn't sure this prayer method was for me. I thought it would be too structured, too forced, too much like a Catholic rosary.

What I discovered, though, as I began to study about praying with Anglican prayer beads and trying out my own prayers, is that it's one of the powerful ways I've ever prayed.

Praying with prayer beads brought more focus and attention to my prayers. Praying this way through Scripture filled my heart with God's Word in a new way. Even though I was praying a formatted prayer, I found I was able to have deeper conversations with God and open my heart more fully to him.

My prayer is that you'll discover a new way to pray and will find a deeper conversation with God this Lent. I pray your heart will be opened and you will discover the power of praying God's Word.

Take it slow, linger in your prayers. As you pray, fill in your own words. Take time to have the hard conversations with God. Open your heart to him and commit to walk closer in his way.

Yours in Christ,
Kathryn Shirey

Special thanks to Beth Sarey for the inspiration and nudging to write this devotional.

Thank you also to my church, St. Philip's Episcopal Church in Frisco, for allowing me to write their Lenten devotional and now share it with you.

Table of Contents

About This Lenten Devotional

What is Lent?

Lent is a season of penitence and repentance leading up to Easter. A season where we recommit our lives to God and turn from the distractions, bad habits, and sins we've accumulated throughout the year and purposefully commit to moving closer to God.

The season of Lent is 40 days (from Ash Wednesday to Easter, not including the Sundays) as a parallel to the 40 days Jesus spent in the wilderness. I've also read that it's about 10% of the year, so like a tithe of our time to refocus on our relationship with God.

How is This Devotional Structured?

This Lenten devotional provides 40 days of daily Scripture readings and prayer guides. On Sundays, enjoy a Sabbath day of spending time with God and your loved ones, go to church, or catch up on a prayer you missed during the week.

40 days can feel like a long time, so don't worry if you miss a day or two (or more). Just pick back up where you left off and keep going!

This devotional is based on the daily readings outlined in the Revised Common Lectionary for the season of Lent.

Other Prayers Included

At the back of this book, you'll find some additional devotionals and prayers.

Two major feast days typically fall within Lent - the Feast of St. Joseph on March 19th and the Feast of the Annunciation on March 25th. Specific devotions for those days have been included in the back of this book, if you want to observe those.

I've also included five prayer guides for using Anglican prayer beads that you can use throughout the year. These include Praying for Others, Praying for Thanksgivings and Blessings, Praying for Strength in the Storm, Praying for Guidance and Direction, and Praying for God's Forgiveness.

What are Anglican Prayer Beads?

Pray with beads? Is that something I should do? But, I'm not Catholic and I'm not sure about praying the rosary.

I'd been getting questions for a while about how to pray with prayer beads, but had resisted the idea. I wasn't sure prayer beads were for me - or were for Protestants for that matter.

Then, when one of the ministry directors at my church asked me to write a Lenten devotional for the church based on praying with Anglican prayer beads I knew I had to dig deeper.

I'm not Catholic, Should I Pray with Prayer Beads?

Turns out, praying with beads is for anyone - even Protestants - and it's become one of my favorite ways to pray.

As I began to pray with prayer beads, I found myself slowing down in my prayers, focusing more on the words I was praying, and spending more quality time with God.

I wasn't as rushed in my prayers.

I brought more scripture to my prayers - and was able to keep those verses with me through the day.

I prayed longer, lingering in my prayers. I found myself wishing for more time to spend in prayer.

Holding the prayers beads was an unexpected blessing, helping pace and guide my prayers, something tangible and tactile to ground my prayers.

What are Anglican Prayer Beads?

Christians have been praying with beads for centuries. The tactile nature of beads helps bring focus to prayers.

While the Catholic rosary has been the most predominant form of prayer with prayer beads, Protestants can also pray with prayer beads.

In the 1980s, an Episcopalian priest in Texas, Rev. Lynn Bauman, created Anglican prayer beads with more Protestant symbolism. While these were originally created for the Episcopal / Anglican tradition, they have been adopted by many Protestants over the years.

These prayer beads start with a cross as a reminder of Christ's act of salvation and includes 33 beads to represent the 33 years of Jesus' life.

The first bead is the largest one, called the Invitatory Bead. This one invites you into prayer, calling God into your presence.

The remaining 32 beads are divided into 4 'weeks'. There are four Cruciform beads to start each week, which are symbolic of the 4 Gospels and the 4 seasons of the year.

Each 'week' includes 7 Week Beads. The number 7 is symbolic of spiritual perfection, 7 days of creation, 7 liturgical seasons of the year, 7 days in the week.

Some may also include a Resurrection Bead next to the Invitatory bead, as a reminder that Christ has triumphed over death and promises us eternal life in his kingdom.

There is no set prayer to use with Anglican prayer beads. Instead, the intent is to use them in any prayer, for any intent. Prayers with prayer beads are most often based on scripture.

Why Pray with Prayer Beads?

Praying with beads adds a tactile component to your prayers. The act of holding the beads and moving from one bead to the next, brings focus to your prayers.

If you struggle to slow down for prayer or feel like you're always rushing through your prayer time, prayer beads are a great way to bring more focus to your prayers.

I've found I spend more time in prayer when I pray with beads and I am more fully present with God. The beads help eliminate the distractions and stray thoughts in my mind. I pray longer, because I'm committed to praying through all the beads.

I also love to use the prayer beads for praying with scripture and have found it helps commit the verse to my heart and my memory through the repetition of the beads.

How To Pray with Anglican Prayer Beads

You can find many prayer guides online and in books for praying with Anglican prayer beads, or you can make your own.

Start by holding the **Cross**, and say an opening prayer.

Next, move to the **Invitatory Bead** and say a prayer to invite God into your presence.

As you enter the circle of weeks beads, say one prayer or scripture at each **Cruciform Bead**.

Next, repeat a small prayer or verse for each of the **Weeks Beads**. Allow the repetition of these prayers to help you pray more deeply and focus more fully.

Go slowly through the beads, allowing some silence between beads. This is a meditative prayer, intended to help you slow down and pray deeper.

You may choose to go around the circle three times, or you can simply go around once.

Return to the **Invitatory Bead** to close your prayers. I personally like to close with the Lord's Prayer at the Invitatory bead.

At the **Cross**, conclude with a simple benediction or say a prayer of your own to respond and reflect on your prayer time.

You can purchase prayer beads at many online stores, including Amazon. Or, you can make your own.

Anglican Prayer Beads

Weeks Beads

Cruciform Beads

Invitatory Bead

Pray around the circle to the right

Cross

How To Use This Devotional

Just a few notes on how this devotional is designed, so you can get the most out of your time.

Set aside 20-30 minutes for your daily devotional, longer if you can. You'll want the time to soak in each day's passages and linger in the prayers.

Read: Begin each day by reading the daily passages. These are from the daily lectionary readings for Lent. Join with millions of others around the world reading these same verses.

Reflect: After you've read the daily passages, spend a few minutes reflecting on what you've read. Use the reflection questions to guide your thoughts. Take a few minutes to journal your thoughts, if you want.

Respond in Prayer:

Next, grab your prayer beads and pray. The symbols will guide you on what parts of the prayer to say with each bead.

I recommend saying these prayers out loud (or even whisper them), so you're not tempted to skim-read. Take time to consider the words as you read and pray, allow the Scripture to soak deeply into your heart as you pray.

Pause between beads to let the prayers sink into your soul and allow God space to enter in.

Prayer Bead Legend:

 Cross - Prayer to say each time you come to the cross.

◯ **Invitatory Bead** - Prayer to say each time you reach the invitatory bead.

∴ **Cruciform Bead** - Prayer to say each time you come to a cruciform bead. If there are four prayers listed, say one for each of the cruciform beads.

● **Weeks Bead** - Prayer to say at each weeks bead. If there are four prayers listed, use one through each set of seven beads.

If you're not praying with prayer beads:
You can still use this devotional if you don't want to pray with prayer beads. Simply pray through the prayers as written in this devotional. You can choose to repeat the prayers designated for the cruciform and weeks beads or just pray them once.

Ash Wednesday

"For where your treasure is, there your heart will be also."
(Matthew 6:21 NIV)

Read: Joel 2:1-2,12-17, Psalm 103, Matthew 6:1-6,16-21

Reflect:

- How will you observe this Lenten season? Will you commit to daily prayer, will you try fasting?
- What most often comes between you and God? How can you fast from that during Lent in order to give God your attention?

Respond in Prayer:

✝ Blow the trumpet in Zion,
   declare a holy fast,
   call a sacred assembly.
Gather the people,
   consecrate the assembly;
bring together the elders,
   gather the children,
   those nursing at the breast.
Let the bridegroom leave his room
   and the bride her chamber.
Let the priests, who minister before the Lord,
   weep between the portico and the altar.
Let them say, "Spare your people, Lord.
   Do not make your inheritance an object of scorn,
   a byword among the nations.
Why should they say among the peoples,
   'Where is their God?'" *(Joel 2:15-17 NIV)*

○ Almighty and everlasting God, you hate nothing you have made and forgive the sins of all who are penitent: Create and make in us new and contrite hearts, that we, worthily lamenting our sins and acknowledging our wretchedness, may obtain of you, the God of all mercy, perfect remission and forgiveness; through Jesus Christ our Lord, who lives and reigns with you and the Holy Spirit, one God, for ever and ever. Amen. *(Collect for Ash Wednesday, BCP)*

cruciform

The Lord is compassionate and gracious,
  slow to anger, abounding in love.
He will not always accuse,
  nor will he harbor his anger forever;
he does not treat me as my sins deserve
  or repay me according to my iniquities. *(Psalm 103:8-10 NIV)*

Praise the Lord, my soul,
  and forget not all his benefits—
who forgives all my sins
  and heals all my diseases,
who redeems my life from the pit
  and crowns me with love and compassion. *(Psalm 103:2-4 NIV)*

Weekly

The Lord's Prayer

We implore you on behalf of Christ, be reconciled to God. For our sake he made him to be sin who knew no sin, so that in him we might become the righteousness of God.

Working together with him, then, we appeal to you not to receive the grace of God in vain. For he says,
  "In a favorable time I listened to you,
    and in a day of salvation I have helped you."

Behold, now is the favorable time; behold, now is the day of salvation. We put no obstacle in anyone's way, so that no fault may be found with our ministry, but as servants of God we commend ourselves in every way: by great endurance, in afflictions, hardships, calamities, beatings, imprisonments, riots, labors, sleepless nights, hunger; by purity, knowledge, patience, kindness, the Holy Spirit, genuine love; by truthful speech, and the power of God; with the weapons of righteousness for the right hand and for the left; through honor and dishonor, through slander and praise. We are treated as impostors, and yet are true; as unknown, and yet well known; as dying, and behold, we live; as punished, and yet not killed; as sorrowful, yet always rejoicing; as poor, yet making many rich; as having nothing, yet possessing everything. *(2 Corinthians 5:20b-6:10 ESV)*

Heavenly and merciful Father, as I enter this season of Lent, I come before you with a humble and penitent heart. I know I don't live the life you desire for me. I know I sin and don't always follow your path. During this season, cleanse my heart and wash away my sin. Make in me a new heart, full of love for you and a desire to more closely walk in your way. Lead me to daily commit to you and give you my full heart. May this be a season of salvation and new life in you. All this I pray through your Son Jesus Christ. Amen.

Thursday After Ash Wednesday

"But what about you?" he asked. "Who do you say I am?"
(Luke 9:20 NIV)

Read: Deuteronomy 30:15-20, Psalm 1, Luke 9:18-25

Reflect:
- Who is Jesus to you?
- What role does he play in your life?
- How will you pick up your cross and follow him?

Respond in Prayer:

✝ Blessed is the one
    who does not walk in step with the wicked
or stand in the way that sinners take
    or sit in the company of mockers,
but whose delight is in the law of the Lord,
    and who meditates on his law day and night.
That person is like a tree planted by streams of water,
    which yields its fruit in season
and whose leaf does not wither—
    whatever they do prospers. *(Psalm 1:1-3 NIV)*

○ Direct us, O Lord, in all our doings with your most gracious favor, and further us with your continual help; in all our works begun, continued, and ended in you, we may glorify your holy Name, and finally, by your mercy, obtain everlasting life; through Jesus Christ our Lord, who lives and reigns with you and the Holy Spirit, one God, for ever and ever. Amen. *(Collect for Thursday after Ash Wednesday, BCP)*

∴ "But who do you say that I am?" "The Christ of God." *(Luke 9:20 ESV)*

❶ I will love the Lord my God with all my heart and with all my soul and with all my strength. *(Deuteronomy 6:5 ESV)*

❷ I will walk in your ways, O God. *(Deuteronomy 30:16 ESV)*

❸ I will follow your commandments. *(Deuteronomy 30:16 ESV)*

❹ I will take up my cross and follow you, Jesus. *(Luke 9:23 ESV)*

⑤ I will forgive
⑥ I will weep ō those who suffer
⑦ I will serve.

The Lord's Prayer

For the LORD knows the way of the righteous,
but the way of the wicked is doomed. *(Psalm 1:6 BCP)*

Jesus, I desire to know you more and seek you with all my heart, mind, and soul. For you are the Messiah, my Savior, and I want to follow you. Direct me to walk in your ways, to follow your commandments, and take up my cross to be your disciple in all that I do. For your path is not the easy one, but it is the one that leads to good things. All this I pray in your name, Amen.

Friday after Ash Wednesday

"Is not this the kind of fasting I chose: to loose the chains of injustice and untie the cords of the yoke to set the oppressed free and break every yoke?" (Isaiah 58:6 NIV)

Read: Isaiah 58:1-9a, Psalm 51:1-10, Matthew 9:10-17

Reflect:
- How will you 'fast' during this Lent season?
- In what ways can you humble yourself during this season in order to draw nearer to God?
- How will you allow God to wash away your sins and help you recommit your ways to him?

Respond in Prayer:

Is this the kind of fast I have chosen,
    only a day for people to humble themselves?
Is it only for bowing one's head like a reed
    and for lying in sackcloth and ashes?
Is that what you call a fast,
    a day acceptable to the Lord?

"Is not this the kind of fasting I have chosen:
to loose the chains of injustice
    and untie the cords of the yoke,
to set the oppressed free
    and break every yoke?
Is it not to share your food with the hungry
    and to provide the poor wanderer with shelter—
when you see the naked, to clothe them,
    and not to turn away from your own flesh and blood?
Then your light will break forth like the dawn,
    and your healing will quickly appear;
then your righteousness[a] will go before you,
    and the glory of the Lord will be your rear guard.
Then you will call, and the Lord will answer;
    you will cry for help, and he will say: Here am I. *(Isaiah 58:5-9a NIV)*

Support us, O Lord, with your gracious favor through the fast we have begun; that as we observe it by bodily self-denial, so we may fulfill it with inner sincerity of heart; through Jesus Christ our Lord, who lives and reigns with you and the Holy Spirit, one God, for ever and ever. Amen. *(Collect for the Friday after Ash Wednesday, BCP)*

Have mercy on me, O God, according to your loving-kindness;
in your great compassion blot out my offenses. *(Psalm 51:1 BCP)*

Wash me through and through from my wickedness
and cleanse me from my sin. *(Psalm 51:2 BCP)*

The Lord's Prayer

And as Jesus reclined at the table in the house, behold, many tax collectors and sinners came and were reclining with Jesus and his disciples. And when the Pharisees saw this, they said to his disciples, "Why does your teacher eat with tax collectors and sinners?" But when he heard it, he said, "Those who are well have no need of a physician, but those who are sick. Go and learn what this means: 'I desire mercy, and not sacrifice.' For I came not to call the righteous, but sinners." *(Matthew 9:10-13 ESV)*

Merciful and gracious Father, show me the ways you want me to honor you through this Lenten season. What do I need to let go of or take up in order to better serve you? Help me to humble myself and fast from the things that keep me from you. Lead me closer to you over these next weeks, washing away my sins and rooting out the bad habits and worldly desires I've taken on. Have mercy on me, a sinner, and in your compassion, heal me as I seek to know you more. Amen.

Saturday After Ash Wednesday

"Those who are well have no need of a physician, but those who are sick. I have not come to call the righteous but sinners to repentance." (Luke 5:31-32 ESV)

Read: Isaiah 58:9b-14, Psalm 86:1-11, Luke 5:27-32

Reflect:
- In what ways do you need healing from Jesus?
- How can you walk closer to his way?
- What parts of your life need the most cleansing and healing How can you use this season of Lent to focus on those with Jesus?

Respond in Prayer:

✝ After this, Jesus went out and saw a tax collector by the name of Levi sitting at his tax booth. "Follow me," Jesus said to him, and Levi got up, left everything and followed him.

Then Levi held a great banquet for Jesus at his house, and a large crowd of tax collectors and others were eating with them. But the Pharisees and the teachers of the law who belonged to their sect complained to his disciples, "Why do you eat and drink with tax collectors and sinners?"

○ Jesus answered them, "It is not the healthy who need a doctor, but the sick. I have not come to call the righteous, but sinners to repentance." *(Luke 5:27-32 NIV)*

Almighty and everlasting God, mercifully look upon our infirmities, and in all our dangers and necessities stretch forth your right hand to help and defend us; through Jesus Christ our Lord, who lives and reigns with you and the Holy Spirit, one God, for ever and ever. Amen
(Collect for the Saturday after Ash Wednesday, BCP)

⋮ Be merciful to me, O Lord, for you are my God;
    I call upon you all the day long.
For you, O Lord, are good and forgiving,
    and great is your love toward all who call upon you. *(Psalm 86:3,5 BCP)*

● Teach me your way, O Lord, and I will walk in your truth;
    knit my heart to you that I may fear your Name. *(Psalm 86:11 BCP)*

○ *The Lord's Prayer*

 Then you will call, and the Lord will answer; you will cry for help, and he will say: Here am I. "If you do away with the yoke of oppression with the pointing finger and malicious talk, and if you spend yourselves in behalf of the hungry and satisfy the needs of the oppressed, then your light will rise in the darkness, and your night will become like the noonday. The Lord will guide you always; he will satisfy your needs in a sun-scorched land and will satisfy your frame. You will be like a well-watered garden, like a sprint whose waters never fail. *(Isaiah 58:9b-11 NIV)*

O Lord, I am in need of your great healing touch. I am a sinner and don't always follow in your way. Heal me, O Lord, in your great mercy and compassion. Teach me your ways and help me to follow where you lead. For great is your love and I know you will answer when I call. Hear my prayers and lead me closer to you. Amen.

Monday in the First Week of Lent

"Who can tell how often he offends? Cleanse me from my secret faults."
(Psalm 19:12 BCP)

Read: Leviticus 19:1-2,11-18, Psalm 19:7-14, Matthew 25:31-46

Reflect:

- Give some serious thought the commandments outlined in the Leviticus passage. Where do you struggle? How can you see each one in your life – either as your own stumbling block or for someone in your life?
- What change do you need to pray for God's help to turn away from the sin or overcome the temptation?

Respond in Prayer:

✠ "Then the righteous will answer him, 'Lord, when did we see you hungry and feed you, or thirsty and give you something to drink? When did we see you a stranger and invite you in, or needing clothes and clothe you? When did we see you sick or in prison and go to visit you?'

"The King will reply, 'Truly I tell you, whatever you did for one of the least of these brothers and sisters of mine, you did for me.' *(Matthew 25:37-40 NIV)*

○ Almighty and everlasting God, mercifully increase in us your gifts of holy discipline, in almsgiving, prayer, and fasting; that our lives may be directed to the fulfilling of your most gracious will; through Jesus Christ our Lord, who lives and reigns with you and the Holy Spirit, one God, for ever and ever. Amen. *(Collect for the Monday in the First Week of Lent, BCP)*

1 You shall not steal; you shall not deal falsely; you shall not lie to one another. You shall not swear by my name falsely, and so profane the name of your God. You shall be holy, for I the Lord your God am holy. *(Leviticus 19:2, 11-12 ESV)*

2 You shall not oppress your neighbor or rob him. The wages of a hired worker shall not remain with you all night until the morning. You shall not curse the deaf or put a stumbling block before the blind, but you shall fear your God. You shall be holy, for I the Lord your God am holy. *(Leviticus 19:2, 13-14 ESV)*

3 You shall do no injustice in court. You shall not be partial to the poor or defer to the great, but in righteousness shall you judge your neighbor. You shall not go around as a slanderer among your people, and you shall not stand up against the life of your neighbor. You shall be holy, for I the Lord your God am holy. *(Leviticus 19:2, 15-16 ESV)*

4 You shall not hate your brother in your heart, but you shall reason frankly with your neighbor, lest you incur sin because of him. You shall not take vengeance or bear a grudge against the sons of your own people, but you shall love your neighbor as yourself. You shall be holy, for I the Lord your God am holy. *(Leviticus 19:2, 17-18 ESV)*

● Who can tell how often he offends?
  cleanse me from my secret faults.
Let the words of my mouth and the meditation of my
  heart be acceptable in your sight,
O Lord, my strength and my redeemer. *(Psalm 19:12, 14 BCP)*

○ *The Lord's Prayer*

✠ The law of the Lord is perfect
  and revives the soul;
  the testimony of the Lord is sure
  and gives wisdom to the innocent.
The statutes of the Lord are just
  and rejoice the heart;
  the commandment of the Lord is clear
  and gives light to the eyes.
The fear of the Lord is clean
  and endures for ever;
  the judgments of the Lord are true
  and righteous altogether.
More to be desired are they than gold,
  more than much fine gold,
  sweeter far than honey,
  than honey in the comb.
By them also is your servant enlightened,
  and in keeping them there is great reward. *(Psalm 19:7-11 BCP)*

Gracious Father, you give us rules out of your great love, to help us live our lives to your glory. Yet, so often I fall short. I'm tempted and sometimes I give in to those temptations. Help me turn from my ways and walk instead in your ways. Show me how to live a life rooted in you, not a life rooted in this world. Open my eyes to see my own sin and help me make the changes I need to make. Lord, have mercy on me. Amen.

Tuesday in the First Week of Lent

"Seek the LORD while he may be found; call on him while he is near"
(Isaiah 55:6 NIV)

Read: Isaiah 55:6–11, Psalm 34:15–22, Matthew 6:7–15

Reflect:

- What are the ways you stay closest to Jesus?
- How is your prayer life? How often do you spend time in prayer? How often do you read your Bible?
- How can you lean into prayer, especially through Lent, to develop a deeper relationship with God?

Respond in Prayer:

And when you pray, do not keep on babbling like pagans, for they think they will be heard because of their many words. Do not be like them, for your Father knows what you need before you ask him.

"This, then, is how you should pray:

"'Our Father in heaven,
hallowed be your name,
your kingdom come,
your will be done,
    on earth as it is in heaven.
Give us today our daily bread.
And forgive us our debts,
    as we also have forgiven our debtors.
And lead us not into temptation,
    but deliver us from the evil one.'

For if you forgive other people when they sin against you, your heavenly Father will also forgive you. But if you do not forgive others their sins, your Father will not forgive your sins. *(Matthew 6:7-15 NIV)*

Grant to your people, Lord, grace to withstand the temptations of the world, the flesh, and the devil, and with pure hearts and minds to follow you, the only true God; through Jesus Christ your Son our Lord, who lives and reigns with you and the Holy Spirit, one God, for ever and ever. Amen. *(Collect for the Tuesday in the First Week of Lent, BCP)*

The Lord is near to the brokenhearted
and will save those whose spirits are crushed.
Many are the troubles of the righteous,
but the Lord will deliver him out of them all. *(Psalm 34:18-19 BCP)*

The righteous cry, and the Lord hears them
and delivers them from all their troubles. *(Psalm 34:17 BCP)*

The Lord's Prayer

For my thoughts are not your thoughts,
neither are your ways my ways, declares the Lord.
For as the heavens are higher than the earth,
so are my ways higher than your ways
and my thoughts than your thoughts.
"For as the rain and the snow come down from heaven
and do not return there but water the earth,
making it bring forth and sprout,
giving seed to the sower and bread to the eater,
so shall my word be that goes out from my mouth;
it shall not return to me empty,
but it shall accomplish that which I purpose,
and shall succeed in the thing for which I sent it. *(Isaiah 55:8-11 ESV)*

O Lord, this world is truly full of temptations, the world calls out to me each step I take. Yet, I desire to follow you. Help me stay rooted in your way and able to withstand the temptations around every corner. Help me to know your Word, reading and studying the Bible. Help me learn to pray – to truly pray and develop a meaningful, personal relationship with you. For you are faithful and good, and you will answer when I call. Amen.

Wednesday in the First Week of Lent

"For as Jonah was a sign to the Ninevites, so also will the Son of Man be to this generation."
(Luke 11:30 NIV)

Read: Jonah 3:1–10, Psalm 51:11–18, Luke 11:29–32

Reflect:
- How are you living in response to Jesus?
- Are you waiting for more signs from God, or is Jesus enough
- How can you be the difference in your world? How can you help spread the good news of Jesus in your family, with your friends, in your work, and elsewhere?

Respond in Prayer:

 Then the word of the Lord came to Jonah a second time: "Go to the great city of Nineveh and proclaim to it the message I give you."

Jonah obeyed the word of the Lord and went to Nineveh. Now Nineveh was a very large city; it took three days to go through it. Jonah began by going a day's journey into the city, proclaiming, "For more days and Nineveh will be overthrown." The Ninevites believed God. A fast was proclaimed, and all of them, from the greatest to the least, put on sackcloth.

When Jonah's warning reached the king of Nineveh, he rose from his throne, took off his royal robes, covered himself with sackcloth and sat down in the dust. This is the proclamation he issued in Nineveh:

"By the decree of the king and his nobles:

Do not let people or animals, herds or flocks, taste anything; do not let them eat or drink. But let people and animals be covered with sackcloth. Let everyone call urgently on God. Let them give up their evil ways and their violence. Who knows? God may yet relent and with compassion turn from his fierce anger so that we will not perish

When God saw what they did and how they turned from their evil ways, he relented and did not bring on them the destruction he had threatened. *(Jonah 3:1-10 NIV)*

○ Bless us, O God, in this holy season, in which our hearts seek your help and healing; and so purify us by your discipline that we may grow in grace and in the knowledge of our Lord and Savior Jesus Christ; who lives and reigns with you and the Holy Spirit, one God, for ever and ever. Amen. *(Collect for the Wednesday in the First Week of Lent, BCP)*

Give me the joy of your saving help again
    and sustain me with your bountiful Spirit.
I shall teach your ways to the wicked,
    and sinners shall return to you.
Open my lips, O Lord,
    and my mouth shall proclaim your praise. *(Psalm 51:13, 14, 16 BCP)*

Create in me a clean heart, O God,
    and renew a right spirit within me. *(Psalm 51:11 BCP)*

○ *The Lord's Prayer*

When the crowds were increasing, he began to say, "This generation is an evil generation. It seeks for a sign, but no sign will be given to it except the sign of Jonah. For as Jonah became a sign to the people of Nineveh, so will the Son of Man be to this generation. The queen of the South will rise up at the judgment with the men of this generation and condemn them, for she came from the ends of the earth to hear the wisdom of Solomon, and behold, something greater than Solomon is here. The men of Nineveh will rise up at the judgment with this generation and condemn it, for they repented at the preaching of Jonah, and behold, something greater than Jonah is here. *(Luke 11:29-32 ESV)*

Heavenly Father, too often I question and wait, wondering how it all matters amidst the world in which I live. Yet, you are enough. You sent your only Son Jesus Christ to earth to live as one of us, to show us the way, and to call us out of our sin and complacency, instead into action to share the good news and lead others to you. Help me to live my life on fire for you and be the change in this world. All this I pray through your Son Jesus Christ. Amen.

Thursday in the First Week of Lent

"Ask and it will be given to you; seek and you will find; knock and the door will be opened to you."
(Matthew 7:7 NIV)

Read: Esther (Apocrypha) 14:1–6,12–14, Psalm 138, Matthew 7:7–12

Reflect:
- What spiritual battles are you fighting in your life today? What afflictions are weighing heavy on your soul?
- Take an honest assessment of your response to these. Do you feel anxiety, depression, despair?
- How can you turn to God instead for strength, courage, and hope against all enemies?

Respond in Prayer:

✠ Queen Esther, seized with deadly anxiety, fled to the Lord. She took off her splendid apparel and put on the garments of distress and mourning, and instead of costly perfumes she covered her head with ashes and dung, and she utterly humbled her body; every part that she loved to adorn she covered with her tangled hair. She prayed to the Lord God of Israel, and said: "O my Lord, you only are our king; help me, who am alone and have no helper but you, for my danger is in my hand. Ever since I was born I have heard in the tribe of my family that you, O Lord, took Israel out of all the nations, and our ancestors from among all their forebears, for an everlasting inheritance, and that you did for them all that you promised. And now we have sinned before you, and you have handed us over to our enemies.

"Remember, O Lord; make yourself known in this time of our affliction, and give me courage, O King of the gods and Master of all dominion! Put eloquent speech in my mouth before the lion, and turn his heart to hate the man who is fighting against us, so that there may be an end of him and those who agree with him. But save us by your hand, and help me, who am alone and have no helper but you, O Lord." *(Esther (Apocrypha) 14:1-6, 12-14 NRSV)*

○ Strengthen us, O Lord, by your grace, that in your might we may overcome all spiritual enemies, and with pure hearts serve you; through Jesus Christ our Lord, who lives and reigns with you and the Holy Spirit, one God, for ever and ever. Amen. *(Collect for the Thursday in the First Week of Lent, BCP)*

I will bow down toward your holy temple
and praise your Name,
because of your love and faithfulness;
When I called, you answered me;
you increased my strength within me. *(Psalm 138:2,4 BCP)*

Though I walk in the midst of trouble, you keep me safe;
you stretch forth your hand against the fury of my enemies;
your right hand shall save me.
The Lord will make good his purpose for me;
O Lord, your love endures for ever; *(Psalm 138:8-9 BCP)*

The Lord's Prayer

"Ask and it will be given to you; seek and you will find; knock and the door will be opened to you. For everyone who asks receives; the one who seeks finds; and to the one who knocks, the door will be opened.

"Which of you, if your son asks for bread, will give him a stone? Or if he asks for a fish, will give him a snake? If you, then, though you are evil, know how to give good gifts to your children, how much more will your Father in heaven give good gifts to those who ask him! So in everything, do to others what you would have them do to you, for this sums up the Law and the Prophets. *(Matthew 7:7-12 NIV)*

Almighty and All-Powerful God, you are bigger than any battle I may fight here on earth. You are more than enough to face the trials in my life. Yet, sometimes the afflictions of this world, the spiritual warfare that rages in my life, seems too much to handle. Remember me and give me courage, O Lord. Fill me with strength and peace and hope against all reason. For you are a giver of good gifts. A Father who lavishes his children with love and will be by my side no matter what the world brings my way. O Lord, have mercy and save me. Amen.

Friday in the First Week of Lent

"But I tell you that anyone who is angry with a brother or sister will be subject to judgement."
(Matthew 5:22 NIV)

Read: Ezekiel 18:21–28, Psalm 130, Matthew 5:20–26

Reflect:
- Where does anger take up residence in your life?
- How does anger come between you and others in your life? Between you and God?
- What steps can you take during this season of Lent to reconcile and set aside the anger?

Respond in Prayer:

✝ "You have heard that it was said to those of old, 'You shall not murder; and whoever murders will be liable to judgment.' But I say to you that everyone who is angry with his brother will be liable to judgment; whoever insults his brother will be liable to the council; and whoever says, 'You fool!' will be liable to the hell of fire. So if you are offering your gift at the altar and there remember that your brother has something against you, leave your gift there before the altar and go. First be reconciled to your brother, and then come and offer your gift. Come to terms quickly with your accuser while you are going with him to court, lest your accuser hand you over to the judge and the judge to the guard, and you be put in prison. Truly, I say to you, you will never get out until you have paid the last penny. *(Matthew 5:21-26 ESV)*

○ Lord Christ, our eternal Redeemer, grant us such fellowship in your sufferings, that, filled with your Holy Spirit, we may subdue the flesh to the spirit, and the spirit to you, and at the last attain to the glory of your resurrection; who lives and reign with the Father and the Holy Spirit, one God, for ever and ever. Amen. *(Collect for the Friday in the First Week of Lent, BCP)*

∴ Out of the depths have I called to you, O Lord;
Lord, hear my voice;
let your ears consider well the voice of my supplication.
If you, Lord, were to note what is done amiss,
O Lord, who could stand?
For there is forgiveness with you;
therefore you shall be feared. *(Psalm 130:1-3 BCP)*

● I wait for the Lord; my soul waits for him;
in his word is my hope.
for with the Lord there is mercy;
With him there is plenteous redemption. *(Psalm 130:4, 6, 7 BCP)*

○ *The Lord's Prayer*

✝ "But if a wicked person turns away from all his sins that he has "But if a wicked person turns away from all the sins they have committed and keeps all my decrees and does what is just and right, that person will surely live; they will not die. None of the offenses they have committed will be remembered against them. Because of the righteous things they have done, they will live. Do I take any pleasure in the death of the wicked? declares the Sovereign Lord. Rather, am I not pleased when they turn from their ways and live?

"But if a righteous person turns from their righteousness and commits sin and does the same detestable things the wicked person does, will they live? None of the righteous things that person has done will be remembered. Because of the unfaithfulness they are guilty of and because of the sins they have committed, they will die.

"Yet you say, 'The way of the Lord is not just.' Hear, you Israelites: Is my way unjust? Is it not your ways that are unjust? If a righteous person turns from their righteousness and commits sin, they will die for it; because of the sin they have committed they will die. But if a wicked person turns away from the wickedness they have committed and does what is just and right, they will save their life. Because they consider all the offenses they have committed and turn away from them, that person will surely live; they will not die. *(Ezekiel 18:21-28 NIV)*

Heavenly Father, help me to root out the anger and resentment in my life. Help me to reconcile with those whom I harbor resentful thoughts or speak toward in anger. For in you there is mercy and hope, even for a sinner like me. Hear my prayers, O Lord, and turn the bitter in my heart into sweet. Teach me how to forgive and let go of age-old anger. Lead me to redemption in you and greater love toward everyone in my life. All this I humbly pray through your Son Jesus Christ. Amen.

Saturday in the First Week of Lent

"But I tell you, love your enemies and pray for those who persecute you."
(Matthew 5:44 NIV)

Read: Deuteronomy 26:16–19, Psalm 119:1–8, Matthew 5:43–48

Reflect:
- Loving your neighbor and hating your enemy is not so hard, but loving your enemies and praying for those who persecute you is hard.
- Where do you need to lean in to better love and pray for those your enemies?
- How can you better reflect the love of Jesus in all that you do?

Respond in Prayer:

✝ "You have heard that it was said, 'Love your neighbor and hate your enemy.' But I tell you, love your enemies and pray for those who persecute you, that you may be children of your Father in heaven. He causes his sun to rise on the evil and the good, and sends rain on the righteous and the unrighteous. If you love those who love you, what reward will you get? Are not even the tax collectors doing that? And if you greet only your own people, what are you doing more than others? Do not even pagans do that? Be perfect, therefore, as your heavenly Father is perfect. *(Matthew 5:43-48 NIV)*

○ O God, by your Word you marvelously carry out the work of reconciliation: Grant that in our Lenten fast we may be devoted to you with all our hearts, and united with one another in prayer and holy love; through Jesus Christ our Lord, who lives and reigns with you and the Holy Spirit, one God, for ever and ever. Amen. *(Collect for the Thursday in the Second Week of Lent, BCP)*

∴ Happy are they whose way is blameless,
   who walk in the law of the Lord!
Happy are they who observe his decrees
   and seek him with all their hearts!
I will thank you with an unfeigned heart,
   when I have learned your righteous judgments.
I will keep your statutes;
   do not utterly forsake me. *(Psalm 119:1-2, 7-8 BCP)*

● You laid down your commandments,
   that we should fully keep them.
Oh, that my ways were made so direct
   that I might keep your statutes! *(Psalm 119:4-5 BCP)*

○ *The Lord's Prayer*

✝ The Lord your God commands you this day to follow these decrees
and laws; carefully observe them with all your heart and with all your
soul. You have declared this day that the Lord is your God and that
you will walk in obedience to him, that you will keep his decrees,
commands and laws—that you will listen to him. And the Lord has
declared this day that you are his people, his treasured possession
as he promised, and that you are to keep all his commands. He has
declared that he will set you in praise, fame and honor high above
all the nations he has made and that you will be a people holy to the
Lord your God, as he promised. *(Deuteronomy 26:16-19 ESV)*

*Jesus, you set such a powerful example of love for us, yet I stumble daily
as I try to live it out in my own life. Show me how to love, to truly love
and pray for those around me, even those who are hard to love. May I
better reflect you and your love in this world. May I learn to set aside
hate and embrace love in all that I do. Have mercy on me and lead me in
your ways. Amen.*

Monday in the Second Week of Lent

"Do to others as you would have them do to you."
(Luke 6:31 NIV)

Read: Daniel 9:3–10, Psalm 79:1–9, Luke 6:27–38

Reflect:

- How is God opening your eyes to your own sin through this Lenten season?
- Where have you been surprised to recognize sin taking hold?
- What sin do you still need to address with God? Will you start that conversation today?

Respond in Prayer:

✝ So I turned to the Lord God and pleaded with him in prayer and petition, in fasting, and in sackcloth and ashes.

I prayed to the Lord my God and confessed:

"Lord, the great and awesome God, who keeps his covenant of love with those who love him and keep his commandments, we have sinned and done wrong. We have been wicked and have rebelled; we have turned away from your commands and laws. We have not listened to your servants the prophets, who spoke in your name to our kings, our princes and our ancestors, and to all the people of the land.

"Lord, you are righteous, but this day we are covered with shame—the people of Judah and the inhabitants of Jerusalem and all Israel, both near and far, in all the countries where you have scattered us because of our unfaithfulness to you. We and our kings, our princes and our ancestors are covered with shame, Lord, because we have sinned against you. The Lord our God is merciful and forgiving, even though we have rebelled against him; we have not obeyed the Lord our God or kept the laws he gave us through his servants the prophets.
(Daniel 9:3-10 NIV)

○ Let your Spirit, O Lord, come into the midst of us to wash us with the pure water of repentance, and prepare us to be always a living sacrifice to you; through Jesus Christ our Lord, who lives and reigns with you and the Holy Spirit, one God, for ever and ever. Amen. *(Collect for the Monday in the Second Week of Lent, BCP)*

∴ "Do not judge, and you will not be judged; do not condemn, and you will not be condemned. Forgive, and you will be forgiven; give, and it will be given to you. For the measure you give will be the measure you get back." *(Luke 6:37-38 NRSV)*

● Help us, O God our Savior, for the glory of your Name; deliver us and forgive us our sins, for your Name's sake. *(Psalm 79:9 BCP)*

○ *The Lord's Prayer*

☦ "But to you who are listening I say: Love your enemies, do good to those who hate you, bless those who curse you, pray for those who mistreat you. If someone slaps you on one cheek, turn to them the other also. If someone takes your coat, do not withhold your shirt from them. Give to everyone who asks you, and if anyone takes what belongs to you, do not demand it back. Do to others as you would have them do to you." *(Luke 6:27-31 ESV)*

Heavenly and almighty Father, I have sinned and done wrong. I don't always recognize the sin in my life, so open my eyes and help me see clearly. Reconcile me to you and lead me to walk in your way, for you are righteous and forgiving. Lord, in your mercy, cleanse me of my sins, open my eyes, and lead me to live as a living sacrifice to you. Amen.

Tuesday in the Second Week of Lent

"Though your sins are like scarlet, they shall be as white as snow;"
(Isaiah 1:18 NIV)

Read: Isaiah 1:2-4,16-20, Matthew 23:1-12, Psalm 50:7-15,22-24

Reflect:
- What sins do you need to ask God to cleanse you from?
- How will turn from the sin in your life and allow God to redeem and renew you?
- How can you be more humble and obedient to God, putting God's Word into practice?

Respond in Prayer:

✝ Wash and make yourselves clean.
   Take your evil deeds out of my sight;
   stop doing wrong.
Learn to do right; seek justice.
   Defend the oppressed.
Take up the cause of the fatherless;
   plead the case of the widow.

"Come now, let us settle the matter,"
   says the Lord.
"Though your sins are like scarlet,
   they shall be as white as snow;
though they are red as crimson,
   they shall be like wool.
If you are willing and obedient,
   you will eat the good things of the land;
but if you resist and rebel,
   you will be devoured by the sword."
For the mouth of the Lord has spoken. *(Isaiah 1:16-20 NIV)*

○ O God, you willed to redeem us from all iniquity by your Son: Deliver us when we are tempted to regard sin without abhorrence, and let the virtue of his passion come between us and our mortal enemy; through Jesus Christ our Lord, who lives and reigns with you and the Holy Spirit, one God, for ever and ever. Amen. *(Collect for the Tuesday in the Second Week of Lent, BCP)*

Consider this well, you who forget God,
   lest I rend you and there be none to deliver you.
Whoever offers me the sacrifice of thanksgiving honors me;
   but to those who keep in my way will I show the salvation of God."
(Psalm 50:23-24 BCP)

Offer to God a sacrifice of thanksgiving
   and make good your vows to the Most High.
Call upon me in the day of trouble;
   I will deliver you, and you shall honor me." *(Psalm 50:14-15 BCP)*

The Lord's Prayer

Then Jesus said to the crowds and to his disciples, "The scribes and the Pharisees sit on Moses' seat, so do and observe whatever they tell you, but not the works they do. For they preach, but do not practice. They tie up heavy burdens, hard to bear, and lay them on people's shoulders, but they themselves are not willing to move them with their finger. They do all their deeds to be seen by others. For they make their phylacteries broad and their fringes long, and they love the place of honor at feasts and the best seats in the synagogues and greetings in the marketplaces and being called rabbi by others. But you are not to be called rabbi, for you have one teacher, and you are all brothers. And call no man your father on earth, for you have one Father, who is in heaven. Neither be called instructors, for you have one instructor, the Christ. The greatest among you shall be your servant. Whoever exalts himself will be humbled, and whoever humbles himself will be exalted. *(Matthew 23:1-12 ESV)*

Heavenly Father, redeem me from my sin. Help me to turn away from my old ways and follow in your way. Though my sins are like scarlet, forgive me and wash them away until they are white as snow. For, I humble myself before you today, confessing my sins and shortcomings, asking your forgiveness. Lord, help me to honor you with my life and follow in your way, May all glory and honor be yours forever. Amen.

Wednesday in the Second Week of Lent

"Like clay in the hand of the potter, so are you in my hand, Israel."
(Jeremiah 18:6 NIV)

Read: Jeremiah 18:1-11,18-20, Psalm 31:9-16, Matthew 20:17-28

Reflect:
- Imagine the clay in the hands of the potter. Visualize how he works and reworks the clay, forming beauty from the mud, remaking broken pieces into works of art.
- How can you place your life in God's hands as the potter with your clay? Imagine how he can reform all your broken pieces into something beautiful.
- Will you let the Great Potter work over your life? Will you trust him and give him control?

Respond in Prayer:

✝ Now Jesus was going up to Jerusalem. On the way, he took the Twelve aside and said to them, "We are going up to Jerusalem, and the Son of Man will be delivered over to the chief priests and the teachers of the law. They will condemn him to death and will hand him over to the Gentiles to be mocked and flogged and crucified. On the third day he will be raised to life!" *(Matthew 20:17-19 ESV)*

○ O God, you so loved the world that you gave your only- begotten Son to reconcile earth with heaven: Grant that we, loving you above all things, may love our friends in you, and our enemies for your sake; through Jesus Christ our Lord, who lives and reigns with you and the Holy Spirit, one God, for ever and ever. Amen. *(Collect for the Wednesday in the Second Week of Lent, BCP)*

⸫ But as for me, I have trusted in you, O Lord.
    I have said, "You are my God.
My times are in your hand;
    rescue me from the hand of my enemies,
    and from those who persecute me.
Make your face to shine upon your servant,
    and in your loving-kindness save me." *(Psalm 31:14-16 BCP)*

● Like clay in the hand of the potter, so am I in your hands, O Lord. *(Jeremiah 18:6 ESV)*

○ *The Lord's Prayer*

✞ Whoever wants to become great among you must be your servant, and whoever wants to be first must be your slave— just as the Son of Man did not come to be served, but to serve, and to give his life as a ransom for many." *(Matthew 20:26-28 ESV)*

O Lord, you are the potter and I am the clay. Take this broken and chipped vessel and remake me into something beautiful and useful to you. I place myself in your hands, give you my control, and release my trust to you. For you can make all things new, you can wash my sins away. You can bind up the broken pieces and use them all to your glory. Make me new, Lord, so that my life may glorify you. Amen.

Thursday in the Second Week of Lent

"That person is like a tree planted by streams of water, which yields its fruit in season and whose leaf does not wither – whatever they do prospers." (Psalm 1:3 NIV)

Read: Jeremiah 17:5–10, Psalm 1, Luke 16:19–31

Reflect:
- What will it take to convince you to repent and follow God?
- Do you need evidence of hell? To hear from those who have gone before you? Or, is Scripture enough?
- How can you firmly root your life in Scripture and the teachings of Jesus in order to remain well-watered by God's streams of life?

Respond in Prayer:

✟ "There was a rich man who was dressed in purple and fine linen and lived in luxury every day. At his gate was laid a beggar named Lazarus, covered with sores and longing to eat what fell from the rich man's table. Even the dogs came and licked his sores.

"The time came when the beggar died and the angels carried him to Abraham's side. The rich man also died and was buried. In Hades, where he was in torment, he looked up and saw Abraham far away, with Lazarus by his side. So he called to him, 'Father Abraham, have pity on me and send Lazarus to dip the tip of his finger in water and cool my tongue, because I am in agony in this fire.'

"But Abraham replied, 'Son, remember that in your lifetime you received your good things, while Lazarus received bad things, but now he is comforted here and you are in agony. And besides all this, between us and you a great chasm has been set in place, so that those who want to go from here to you cannot, nor can anyone cross over from there to us.'

"He answered, 'Then I beg you, father, send Lazarus to my family, for I have five brothers. Let him warn them, so that they will not also come to this place of torment.'

"Abraham replied, 'They have Moses and the Prophets; let them listen to them.'

"'No, father Abraham,' he said, 'but if someone from the dead goes to them, they will repent.'

"He said to him, 'If they do not listen to Moses and the Prophets, they will not be convinced even if someone rises from the dead.'"
(Luke 16:19-31 NIV)

○ O Lord, strong and mighty, Lord of hosts and King of glory: Cleanse our hearts from sin, keep our hands pure, and turn our minds from what is passing away; so that at the last we may stand in your holy place and receive your blessing; through Jesus Christ our Lord, who lives and reigns with you and the Holy Spirit, one God, for ever and ever. Amen. *(Collect for the Thursday in the Second Week of Lent, BCP)*

Happy are they who have not walked in the counsel of the wicked,
    nor lingered in the way of sinners,
    nor sat in the seats of the scornful!
Their delight is in the law of the Lord,
    and they meditate on his law day and night.
They are like trees planted by streams of water,
    bearing fruit in due season, with leaves that do not wither;
    everything they do shall prosper. *(Psalm 1:1-3 BCP)*

● Cursed is the one who trusts in man,
    who draws strength from mere flesh
    and whose heart turns away from the Lord.
But blessed is the one who trusts in the Lord,
    whose confidence is in him. *(Jeremiah 17:5,7 ESV)*

○ *The Lord's Prayer*

✝ "Cursed is the one who trusts in man,
    who draws strength from mere flesh
    and whose heart turns away from the Lord.
That person will be like a bush in the wastelands;
    they will not see prosperity when it comes.
They will dwell in the parched places of the desert,
    in a salt land where no one lives.
"But blessed is the one who trusts in the Lord,
    whose confidence is in him.
They will be like a tree planted by the water
    that sends out its roots by the stream.
It does not fear when heat comes;
    its leaves are always green.
It has no worries in a year of drought
    and never fails to bear fruit." *(Jeremiah 17:5-8 ESV)*

Almighty Father, Gracious God, hear my prayer. Keep me firmly planted in your true soil, watered by your streams of living water. Teach me your ways and open my heart to hear and understand your Word. Help me commit to reading and studying the Bible. Firmly plant me with others who are committed to you, who will show me the way. May I always know that you are enough, more than the world can ever offer. And, may I ever desire to walk only in your way, to your glory. Amen.

Friday in the Second Week of Lent

"Therefore I tell you that the kingdom of God will be taken away from you and given to a people wh[o] will produce its fruit." (Matthew 21:43 NIV)

Read: Genesis 37:3–4,12–28, Psalm 105:16–22, Matthew 21:33–43

Reflect:
- How are you showing grace to others in your life?
- To whom do you need to show more grace? Where do you need to work on forgiveness?
- How can you produce more fruit with what God has entrusted to your care?

Respond in Prayer:

✝ "Listen to another parable: There was a landowner who planted a vineyard. He put a wall around it, dug a winepress in it and built a watchtower. Then he rented the vineyard to some farmers and moved to another place. When the harvest time approached, he sen[t] his servants to the tenants to collect his fruit.

"The tenants seized his servants; they beat one, killed another, and stoned a third. Then he sent other servants to them, more than the first time, and the tenants treated them the same way. Last of all, he sent his son to them. 'They will respect my son,' he said.

"But when the tenants saw the son, they said to each other, 'This is the heir. Come, let's kill him and take his inheritance.' So they took him and threw him out of the vineyard and killed him.

"Therefore, when the owner of the vineyard comes, what will he do to those tenants?"

"He will bring those wretches to a wretched end," they replied, "and he will rent the vineyard to other tenants, who will give him his shar[e] of the crop at harvest time." *(Matthew 21:33-41 NIV)*

○ Grant, O Lord, that as your Son Jesus Christ prayed for his enemies on the cross, so we may have grace to forgive those who wrongfully or scornfully use us, that we ourselves may be able to receive your forgiveness; through Jesus Christ our Lord, who lives and reigns with you and the Holy Spirit, one God, for ever and ever. Amen. *(Collect for the Friday in the Second Week of Lent, BCP)*

Remember the wonders he has done,
    his miracles, and the judgments he pronounced,
you his servants, the descendants of Abraham,
    his chosen ones, the children of Jacob.
He is the Lord our God;
    his judgments are in all the earth. *(Psalm 105:5-7 ESV)*

I will look to the Lord and his strength
    I will seek his face always. *(Psalm 105:4 ESV)*

The Lord's Prayer

Jesus said to them, "Have you never read in the Scriptures:

"'The stone the builders rejected
    has become the cornerstone;
the Lord has done this,
    and it is marvelous in our eyes'?

"Therefore I tell you that the kingdom of God will be taken away from you and given to a people who will produce its fruit. *(Matthew 21:42-43 NIV)*

O Lord, you have entrusted me with so much. How can I be more fruitful in my relationships, the use of my gifts and talents, and in my faith? Show me where I can do more to love those in my life and have a forgiving heart. Open my eyes to see where I can better use my gifts for your glory. Help me to live a life that better reflects you. All this I pray through your Son Jesus, who taught us by his words and his actions how to love well. Amen.

Saturday in the Second Week of Lent

"'My son,' the father said, 'you are always with me, and everything I have is yours. But we had to celebrate and be glad, because this brother of yours was dead and is alive again; he was lost and is found.'" (Luke 15:31-32 NIV)

Read: Micah 7:14-15,18-20, Psalm 103:1-12, Luke 15:11-32

Reflect:

- As you reflect over the parable of the prodigal son, with whom do you most identify? Are you the son who left and desired to come back? Are you the son who stayed and feel resentment over the celebration of the prodigal's return?
- If you feel like the prodigal son, consider how you can return home? Return to God's home? Will you take the first step so that God can welcome you back with open arms and great celebration?
- If you feel like the son who stayed faithful to his father, how can you find joy and contentment in the comfort of God? Can you celebrate over the prodigal's return, knowing you've been when you needed to be all along?

Respond in Prayer:

✝ Who is a God like you,
  who pardons sin and forgives the transgression
  of the remnant of his inheritance?
You do not stay angry forever
  but delight to show mercy.
You will again have compassion on us;
  you will tread our sins underfoot
  and hurl all our iniquities into the depths of the sea.
You will be faithful to Jacob,
  and show love to Abraham,
as you pledged on oath to our ancestors
  in days long ago. *(Micah 7:18-20 ESV)*

○ Grant, most merciful Lord, to your faithful people pardon and peace, that they may be cleansed from all their sins, and serve you with a quiet mind; through Jesus Christ our Lord, who lives and reigns with you and the Holy Spirit, one God, for ever and ever. Amen. *(Collect for the Saturday in the Second Week of Lent, BCP)*

For as the heavens are high above the earth,
  so is his mercy great upon those who fear him.
As far as the east is from the west,
  so far has he removed our sins from us. *(Psalm 103: 11-12 BCP)*

He has redeemed my life from the pit
  and crowned me with love and compassion. *(Psalm 103:4 BCP)*

The Lord's Prayer

"The older brother became angry and refused to go in. So his father went out and pleaded with him. But he answered his father, 'Look! All these years I've been slaving for you and never disobeyed your orders. Yet you never gave me even a young goat so I could celebrate with my friends. But when this son of yours who has squandered your property with prostitutes comes home, you kill the fattened calf for him!'

"'My son,' the father said, 'you are always with me, and everything I have is yours. But we had to celebrate and be glad, because this brother of yours was dead and is alive again; he was lost and is found.'" *(Luke 15:28-32 ESV)*

Lord, thank you for your open arms and forgiving heart, welcoming me back when I've strayed and loving me when I've stayed. I love that you're never too far away, that you've always loved me no matter where I've wandered. Bring me home to your loving arms. Keep me firmly in your grasp. Don't let me be lost anymore. For I want to seek you and find you, remaining in your loving embrace the rest of my days. Amen.

Monday in the Third Week of Lent

As the deer pants for streams of water, so my soul pants for you, my God.
(Psalm 42:1 NIV)

Read: 2 Kings 5:1–15b, Luke 4:23–30, Psalm 42

Reflect:
- Are you praying for answers, but not trusting in God's solutions?
- Are you wishing for God's power or do you know in your heart that he has all power and might in this world?
- How can you more fully trust in God's way and God's time?
- Today, pray to put trust in God, releasing your soul to long for more of God in your life.

Respond in Prayer:

✝ Have the man come to me and he will know that there is a prophet in Israel." So Naaman went with his horses and chariots and stopped at the door of Elisha's house. Elisha sent a messenger to say to him, "Go, wash yourself seven times in the Jordan, and your flesh will be restored and you will be cleansed."

But Naaman went away angry and said, "I thought that he would surely come out to me and stand and call on the name of the Lord his God, wave his hand over the spot and cure me of my leprosy. Are not Abana and Pharpar, the rivers of Damascus, better than all the waters of Israel? Couldn't I wash in them and be cleansed?" So he turned and went off in a rage.

Naaman's servants went to him and said, "My father, if the prophet had told you to do some great thing, would you not have done it? How much more, then, when he tells you, 'Wash and be cleansed'!" So he went down and dipped himself in the Jordan seven times, as the man of God had told him, and his flesh was restored and became clean like that of a young boy.

Then Naaman and all his attendants went back to the man of God. He stood before him and said, "Now I know that there is no God in all the world except in Israel. *(2 Kings 5:8b-15b NIV)*

○ Look upon the heart-felt desires of your humble servants, Almighty God, and stretch forth the right hand of your majesty to be our defense against all our enemies; through Jesus Christ our Lord, who lives and reigns with you and the Holy Spirit, one God, for ever and ever. Amen. *(Collect for the Monday in the Third Week of Lent, BCP)*

∴ Put your trust in God;
  for I will yet give thanks to him,
  who is the help of my countenance, and my God. *(Psalm 42:7 BCP)*

● As the deer longs for the water-brooks,
  so longs my soul for you, O God. *(Psalm 42:1 BCP)*

○ *The Lord's Prayer*

☦ And he said to them, "Doubtless you will quote to me this proverb, "'Physician, heal yourself.' What we have heard you did at Capernaum, do here in your hometown as well.'" And he said, "Truly, I say to you, no prophet is acceptable in his hometown. But in truth, I tell you, there were many widows in Israel in the days of Elijah, when the heavens were shut up three years and six months, and a great famine came over all the land, and Elijah was sent to none of them but only to Zarephath, in the land of Sidon, to a woman who was a widow. And there were many lepers in Israel in the time of the prophet Elisha, and none of them was cleansed, but only Naaman the Syrian." When they heard these things, all in the synagogue were filled with wrath. And they rose up and drove him out of the town and brought him to the brow of the hill on which their town was built, so that they could throw him down the cliff. But passing through their midst, he went away. *(Luke 4:23-30 ESV)*

O Holy Lord, may I ever trust in you and in your ways. For you are mighty and powerful, the beginning and the end, the ruler over heaven and earth. My soul longs for more of you in my life, O Lord, so I will place my hope and my trust in you. For you are my rock and my defense, my shelter and my salvation. I give thanks and praise today for you and for your love. Amen.

Tuesday in the Third Week of Lent

"They saw that the fire had not harmed their bodies, nor was a hair of their heads singed; their robe were not scorched, and there was no smell of fire on them." (Daniel 3:27 NIV)

Read: Daniel 3:19-29, Psalm 25:3-10, Matthew 18:21-35

Reflect:

- When you're walking through seasons of great adversity, to whom do you turn?
- What settles in your heart as you face great trials in your lif Do you have a heart full of praise for a God in whom you trust? Or, do you feel despair and overwhelm, uncertain of where you'll find the strength for the road ahead?
- How can you have the faith of Shadrach, Meshach and Abednego, to face the fiery trials in your own life and trust that God can bring you through unsinged?

Respond in Prayer:

✝ Nebuchadnezzar then approached the opening of the blazing furnac and shouted, "Shadrach, Meshach and Abednego, servants of the Most High God, come out! Come here!"

So Shadrach, Meshach and Abednego came out of the fire, and the satraps, prefects, governors and royal advisers crowded around ther They saw that the fire had not harmed their bodies, nor was a hair o their heads singed; their robes were not scorched, and there was no smell of fire on them.

Then Nebuchadnezzar said, "Praise be to the God of Shadrach, Meshach and Abednego, who has sent his angel and rescued his servants! They trusted in him and defied the king's command and were willing to give up their lives rather than serve or worship any god except their own God. Therefore I decree that the people of any nation or language who say anything against the God of Shadrach, Meshach and Abednego be cut into pieces and their houses be turned into piles of rubble, for no other god can save in this way." *(Daniel 3:26-29 NIV)*

○ O Lord, we beseech you mercifully to hear us; and grant that we, to whom you have given a fervent desire to pray, may, by your mighty aid, be defended and comforted in all dangers and adversities; through Jesus Christ our Lord, who lives and reigns with you and th Holy Spirit, one God, for ever and ever. Amen. *(Collect for the Tuesday in th Third Week of Lent, BCP)*

Lead me in your truth and teach me,
    for you are the God of my salvation;
    in you have I trusted all the day long.
Remember not the sins of my youth and my transgressions;
    remember me according to your love
    and for the sake of your goodness, O Lord. *(Psalm 25:4,6 BCP)*

Show me your ways, O Lord,
    and teach me your paths. *(Psalm 25:3 BCP)*

The Lord's Prayer

And they walked about in the midst of the flames, singing hymns to God and blessing the Lord. Then Azari'ah stood and offered this prayer; in the midst of the fire he opened his mouth and said:

"Blessed art thou, O Lord, God of our fathers, and worthy of praise;
    and thy name is glorified for ever.
For thou art just in all that thou hast done to us,
    and all thy works are true and thy ways right,
    and all thy judgments are truth.

Yet with a contrite heart and a humble spirit may we be accepted,
    as though it were with burnt offerings of rams and bulls,
    and with tens of thousands of fat lambs;
    such may our sacrifice be in thy sight this day,
    and may we wholly follow thee,
    for there will be no shame for those who trust in thee.
And now with all our heart we follow thee,
    we fear thee and seek thy face.
Do not put us to shame,
    but deal with us in thy forbearance
    and in thy abundant mercy.
Deliver us in accordance with thy marvelous works,
    and give glory to thy name, O Lord!
(Song of the Three Young Men 1-4, 16-20 RSV)

O God, Most High, for whom nothing is impossible. Walk with me through the fire, be by my side through the trials of this life. Send your angels to shelter and protect me, to fight the battles on my behalf. For you are mightier than any human affliction, more powerful than enemy I will face. I will put my trust in you and sing your praises through the storm. Protect me and defend me. Give me shelter and support. Lead me and I will follow. Amen.

Wednesday in the Third Week of Lent

"Do not add to what I command you and do not subtract from it, but keep the commands of the Lord your God that I give you." (Deuteronomy 4:2 NIV)

Read: Deuteronomy 4:1-2,5-9, Psalm 78:1-6, Matthew 5:17-19

Reflect:
- How often do you read and study the Bible? How well do you know its teachings?
- How important is the Bible in your life?
- What steps can you take to know it better? How can you share it with others in your life, especially with the younger generations?

Respond in Prayer:

✝ "And now, O Israel, listen to the statutes and the rules that I am teaching you, and do them, that you may live, and go in and take possession of the land that the Lord, the God of your fathers, is giving you. You shall not add to the word that I command you, nor take from it, that you may keep the commandments of the Lord your God that I command you.

See, I have taught you statutes and rules, as the Lord my God commanded me, that you should do them in the land that you are entering to take possession of it. Keep them and do them, for that will be your wisdom and your understanding in the sight of the peoples, who, when they hear all these statutes, will say, 'Surely this great nation is a wise and understanding people.' For what great nation is there that has a god so near to it as the Lord our God is to us, whenever we call upon him? And what great nation is there, that has statutes and rules so righteous as all this law that I set before you today?

"Only take care, and keep your soul diligently, lest you forget the things that your eyes have seen, and lest they depart from your heart all the days of your life. Make them known to your children and your children's children— *(Deuteronomy 4:1-2,5-9 ESV)*

○ Give ear to our prayers, O Lord, and direct the way of your servants safety under your protection, that, amid all the changes of our earthly pilgrimage, we may be guarded by your mighty aid; through Jesus Christ our Lord, who lives and reigns with you and the Holy Spirit, one God, for ever and ever. Amen. *(Collect for the Wednesday in the Third Week of Lent, BCP)*

∴ I will recount to generations to come
the praiseworthy deeds and the power of the Lord,
and the wonderful works he has done. *(Psalm 78:4 BCP)*

● I will hear your teaching, O Lord;
I will incline my ears to the words of your mouth. *(Psalm 78:1 BCP)*

○ *The Lord's Prayer*

✝ "Do not think that I have come to abolish the Law or the Prophets; I have not come to abolish them but to fulfill them. For truly, I say to you, until heaven and earth pass away, not an iota, not a dot, will pass from the Law until all is accomplished. Therefore whoever relaxes one of the least of these commandments and teaches others to do the same will be called least in the kingdom of heaven, but whoever does them and teaches them will be called great in the kingdom of heaven. *(Matthew 5:17-19 ESV)*

O Lord, open my ears to hear your teaching, open my eyes to see your truth. Lead me as I read and study your Word. Guide me as I seek your rule. For your statutes and commandments are given out of your great love for us, to guide us and teach us how to live and serve you best. Teach me, Lord, and I will in turn teach others. Make known to me your will and lead me to follow your way. Amen.

Thursday in the Third Week of Lent

"Whoever is not with me is against me, and whoever does not gather with me scatters."
(Luke 11:23 NIV)

Read: Jeremiah 7:23–28, Psalm 95:6–11, Luke 11:14–23

Reflect:
- Today, pray for the church as a whole, that we may all walk more closely together in God's love and continue the work of bringing more of God's Kingdom here on earth.
- How can you support and pray for your local church?
- How can you support and pray for the global body of Christ?
- When Jesus says, "Whoever is not with me is against me, and whoever does not gather with me scatters," how does that apply to you? To the church at large?

Respond in Prayer:

✝ But I gave them this command: Obey me, and I will be your God and you will be my people. Walk in obedience to all I command you, that it may go well with you. But they did not listen or pay attention; instead, they followed the stubborn inclinations of their evil hearts. They went backward and not forward. From the time your ancestors left Egypt until now, day after day, again and again I sent you my servants the prophets. But they did not listen to me or pay attention. They were stiff-necked and did more evil than their ancestors.'

"When you tell them all this, they will not listen to you; when you call to them, they will not answer. Therefore say to them, 'This is the nation that has not obeyed the Lord its God or responded to correction. Truth has perished; it has vanished from their lips. *(Jeremiah 7:23-28 NIV)*

○ Keep watch over your Church, O Lord, with your unfailing love; and, since it is grounded in human weakness and cannot maintain itself without your aid, protect it from all danger, and keep it in the way of salvation; through Jesus Christ your Son our Lord, who lives and reigns with you and the Holy Spirit, one God, for ever and ever. Amen
(Collect for the Thursday in the Third Week of Lent, BCP)

Oh come, let us sing to the Lord;
  let us make a joyful noise to the rock of our salvation!
Let us come into his presence with thanksgiving;
  let us make a joyful noise to him with songs of praise!
For the Lord is a great God,
  and a great King above all gods.
In his hand are the depths of the earth;
  the heights of the mountains are his also.
The sea is his, for he made it,
  and his hands formed the dry land. *(Psalm 95:1-5 ESV)*

Oh come, let us worship and bow down;
  let us kneel before the Lord, our Maker!
For he is our God,
  and we are the people of his pasture,
  and the sheep of his hand. *(Psalm 95:6-7 ESV)*

The Lord's Prayer

Now he was casting out a demon that was mute. When the demon had gone out, the mute man spoke, and the people marveled. But some of them said, "He casts out demons by Beelzebul, the prince of demons," while others, to test him, kept seeking from him a sign from heaven. But he, knowing their thoughts, said to them, "Every kingdom divided against itself is laid waste, and a divided household falls. And if Satan also is divided against himself, how will his kingdom stand? For you say that I cast out demons by Beelzebul. And if I cast out demons by Beelzebul, by whom do your sons cast them out? Therefore they will be your judges. But if it is by the finger of God that I cast out demons, then the kingdom of God has come upon you. When a strong man, fully armed, guards his own palace, his goods are safe; but when one stronger than he attacks him and overcomes him, he takes away his armor in which he trusted and divides his spoil. Whoever is not with me is against me, and whoever does not gather with me scatters. *(Luke 11:14-23 ESV)*

O Lord Almighty, watch over your church and lead us closer to you and living out your mission. Protect the body of believers from all the dangers, temptations, and persecution that lead us from you. Protect the church from its own weaknesses and faults, building it up to lead through love as you love us. We need you, O Lord, to strengthen the church at home and across the world, so we can shine your powerful light in this dark world and bring glory to you. All this I pray through your Son Jesus Christ. Amen.

Friday in the Third Week of Lent

"The most important one," answered Jesus, "is this: 'Hear, O Israel: The Lord your God, the Lord is O[...] Love the Lord your God with all your heart and with all your soul and with all your mind and with a[...] your strength.'" (Mark 12:29-30 NIV)

Read: Hosea 14:1–9, Psalm 81:8–14, Mark 12:28–34

Reflect:

- Today, take an honest assessment of the idols in your life. Where do you place your value? What Earthly goods and goals sit atop your priority list?
- Where is God on your life? How are you loving him above a[...] else, with all your heart, and with all your soul, and all your mind, and with all your strength?
- Pray today about what needs in your life to remove the ido[...] and place God alone at the top of your priorities?

Respond in Prayer:

✝ And one of the scribes came up and heard them disputing with one another, and seeing that he answered them well, asked him, "Which commandment is the most important of all?" Jesus answered, "The most important is, 'Hear, O Israel: The Lord our God, the Lord is one[...] And you shall love the Lord your God with all your heart and with all your soul and with all your mind and with all your strength.' The second is this: 'You shall love your neighbor as yourself.' There is no other commandment greater than these." And the scribe said to him[...] "You are right, Teacher. You have truly said that he is one, and there is no other besides him. And to love him with all the heart and with all the understanding and with all the strength, and to love one's neighbor as oneself, is much more than all whole burnt offerings an[...] sacrifices." And when Jesus saw that he answered wisely, he said to him, "You are not far from the kingdom of God." And after that no o[...] dared to ask him any more questions. *(Mark 12:28-34 ESV)*

○ Grant us, O Lord our Strength, a true love of your holy Name; so tha[...] trusting in your grace, we may fear no earthly evil, nor fix our hearts on earthly goods, but may rejoice in your full salvation; through Jesu[...] Christ our Lord, who lives and reigns with you and the Holy Spirit, one God, for ever and ever. Amen. *(Collect for the Friday in the Third Week of Lent, BCP)*

"If my people would only listen to me,
  if Israel would only follow my ways,
how quickly I would subdue their enemies
  and turn my hand against their foes!
Those who hate the Lord would cringe before him,
  and their punishment would last forever.
But you would be fed with the finest of wheat;
  with honey from the rock I would satisfy you." *(Psalm 81:13-16 NIV)*

"You shall have no foreign god among you;
  you shall not worship any god other than me," says the Lord your
God. *(Psalm 81:9 NIV)*

The Lord's Prayer

"I will heal their waywardness
  and love them freely,
  for my anger has turned away from them.
I will be like the dew to Israel;
  he will blossom like a lily.
Like a cedar of Lebanon
  he will send down his roots;
  his young shoots will grow.
His splendor will be like an olive tree,
  his fragrance like a cedar of Lebanon.
People will dwell again in his shade;
  they will flourish like the grain,
they will blossom like the vine—
  Israel's fame will be like the wine of Lebanon.
Ephraim, what more have I to do with idols?
  I will answer him and care for him.
I am like a flourishing juniper;
  your fruitfulness comes from me."

Who is wise? Let them realize these things.
  Who is discerning? Let them understand.
The ways of the Lord are right;
  the righteous walk in them,
  but the rebellious stumble in them. *(Hosea 14:4-9 NIV)*

Heavenly Father, Lord Almighty, forgive me for chasing worldly goals and earthly goods. Help me instead to love you fully – with all my heart, with all my soul, with all my mind, and with all my strength. Help me keep you at the top of my priorities, trusting in you for all my needs and all my worth. For you alone are enough for me. May I ever hear your voice and obey your commands. Lord, have mercy on me and grant me the strength to step out in faith. Amen.

Saturday in the Third Week of Lent

"For all those who exalt themselves will be humbled, and those who humble themselves will be exalted." (Luke 18:14 NIV)

Read: Hosea 6:1–6, Psalm 51:15–20, Luke 18:9–14

Reflect:

- What are the temptations in your life? Where do you too often fall short of God's desire for your life?
- Admitting our sins and temptations is humbling, but not one of us is perfect. We're human and we sin.
- Like the tax collector in the Luke passage, will you come before God today and pray for mercy and forgiveness? Ask for God's help in the areas you struggle the most.

Respond in Prayer:

✝ To some who were confident of their own righteousness and looked down on everyone else, Jesus told this parable: "Two men went up to the temple to pray, one a Pharisee and the other a tax collector. The Pharisee stood by himself and prayed: 'God, I thank you that I am not like other people—robbers, evildoers, adulterers—or even like this tax collector. I fast twice a week and give a tenth of all I get.'

"But the tax collector stood at a distance. He would not even look up to heaven, but beat his breast and said, 'God, have mercy on me, a sinner.'

"I tell you that this man, rather than the other, went home justified before God. For all those who exalt themselves will be humbled, and those who humble themselves will be exalted." *(Luke 18:9-14 NIV)*

○ O God, you know us to be set in the midst of so many and great dangers, that by reason of the frailty of our nature we cannot always stand upright: Grant us such strength and protection as may support us in all dangers, and carry us through all temptations; through Jesus Christ our Lord, who lives and reigns with you and the Holy Spirit, one God, for ever and ever. Amen. *(Collect for the Saturday in the Third Week of Lent, BCP)*

Cleanse me with hyssop, and I will be clean;
    wash me, and I will be whiter than snow.
Let me hear joy and gladness;
    let the bones you have crushed rejoice.
Hide your face from my sins
    and blot out all my iniquity. *(Psalm 51:7-9 NIV)*

My sacrifice, O God, is a broken spirit;
    a broken and contrite heart
    you, God, will not despise. *(Psalm 51:17 NIV)*

The Lord's Prayer

"Come, let us return to the Lord;
    for he has torn us, that he may heal us;
    he has struck us down, and he will bind us up.
After two days he will revive us;
    on the third day he will raise us up,
    that we may live before him.
Let us know; let us press on to know the Lord;
    his going out is sure as the dawn;
he will come to us as the showers,
    as the spring rains that water the earth." *(Hosea 6:1-3 ESV)*

Most Merciful Father, forgive me of my sins. Have mercy on me, a sinner, who too often falls for the temptations that call out to me daily. Today, I humbly come before you and admit these areas where I fall short and sin, and ask for your help to turn back to your path and follow in your way. Lord, have mercy and forgive me. Amen.

Monday in the Fourth Week of Lent

"But be glad and rejoice forever in what I will create, for I will create Jerusalem to be a delight and its people a joy." (Isaiah 65:18 NIV)

Read: Isaiah 65:17–25, Psalm 30:1–6,11–13, John 4:43–54

Reflect:
- What great things is God doing in your life? How do you recognize the areas where God is at work around you?
- Where do you see God bringing forth joy from sadness, life from death, hope from despair?
- Pray today to have your eyes opened to see God's great gifts and to trust in his great ways.

Respond in Prayer:

✝ After the two days he left for Galilee. (Now Jesus himself had pointed out that a prophet has no honor in his own country.) When he arrived in Galilee, the Galileans welcomed him. They had seen all that he had done in Jerusalem at the Passover Festival, for they also had been there.

Once more he visited Cana in Galilee, where he had turned the water into wine. And there was a certain royal official whose son lay sick at Capernaum. When this man heard that Jesus had arrived in Galilee from Judea, he went to him and begged him to come and heal his son who was close to death.

"Unless you people see signs and wonders," Jesus told him, "you will never believe."

The royal official said, "Sir, come down before my child dies."

"Go," Jesus replied, "your son will live."

The man took Jesus at his word and departed. While he was still on the way, his servants met him with the news that his boy was living. When he inquired as to the time when his son got better, they said to him, "Yesterday, at one in the afternoon, the fever left him."

Then the father realized that this was the exact time at which Jesus had said to him, "Your son will live." So he and his whole household believed.

This was the second sign Jesus performed after coming from Judea to Galilee. *(John 4:43-54 NIV)*

O Lord our God, in your holy Sacraments you have given us a foretaste of the good things of your kingdom: Direct us, we pray, in the way that leads to eternal life, that we may come to appear before you in that place of light where you dwell for ever with your saints; through Jesus Christ our Lord, who lives and reigns with you and the Holy Spirit, one God, for ever and ever. Amen. *(Collect for the Monday in the Fourth Week of Lent, BCP)*

Hear, O Lord, and have mercy upon me;
    O Lord, be my helper."
You have turned my wailing into dancing;
    you have put off my sack-cloth and clothed me with joy.
Therefore my heart sings to you without ceasing;
    O Lord my God, I will give you thanks for ever. *(Psalm 30:11-13 BCP)*

I will exalt you, O Lord,
    because you have lifted me up
    and have not let my enemies triumph over me. *(Psalm 30:1 BCP)*

The Lord's Prayer

"For behold, I create new heavens
    and a new earth,
and the former things shall not be remembered
    or come into mind.
But be glad and rejoice forever
    in that which I create;
for behold, I create Jerusalem to be a joy,
    and her people to be a gladness.
Before they call I will answer;
    while they are yet speaking I will hear.
The wolf and the lamb shall graze together;
    the lion shall eat straw like the ox,
    and dust shall be the serpent's food.
They shall not hurt or destroy
    in all my holy mountain,"
says the Lord. *(Isaiah 65:17-18,24-25 ESV)*

Heavenly Father, I give thanks and praise today for all of your great works. Thank you for all the ways you bless us, giving us your best. Open my eyes so I may see the ways you bring forth joy from sadness, life from death, hope from despair. May I keep my eyes focused on the blessings and wonders of your love, instead of focused on the trials of this world. Make in me a new heart, full of gladness and joy. Amen.

Tuesday in the Fourth Week of Lent

Then Jesus said to him, "Get up! Pick up your mat and walk." At once the man was cured; he picked his mat and walked." (John 5:8-9 NIV)

Read: Ezekiel 47:1–9,12, Psalm 46:1–8, John 5:1–18

Reflect:

- Jesus asked the man by the pool, "Do you want to be healed?" The man responded with all the practical reasons (and maybe even excuses) he couldn't reach the healing waters.
- What about you? Do you want to be healed by the Living Water of Jesus?
- What's holding you back from stepping into the waters?

Respond in Prayer:

✝ Some time later, Jesus went up to Jerusalem for one of the Jewish festivals. Now there is in Jerusalem near the Sheep Gate a pool, which in Aramaic is called Bethesda and which is surrounded by five covered colonnades. Here a great number of disabled people used to lie—the blind, the lame, the paralyzed. One who was there had been an invalid for thirty-eight years. When Jesus saw him lying there and learned that he had been in this condition for a long time, he asked him, "Do you want to get well?"

"Sir," the invalid replied, "I have no one to help me into the pool when the water is stirred. While I am trying to get in, someone else goes down ahead of me."

Then Jesus said to him, "Get up! Pick up your mat and walk." At once the man was cured; he picked up his mat and walked.

The day on which this took place was a Sabbath, *(John 5:1-9 NIV)*

○ O God, with you is the well of life, and in your light we see light: Quench our thirst with living water, and flood our darkened minds with heavenly light; through Jesus Christ our Lord, who lives and reigns with you and the Holy Spirit, one God, for ever and ever. Amen *(Collect for the Tuesday in the Fourth Week of Lent, BCP)*

There is a river whose streams make glad the city of God,
the holy habitation of the Most High.
God is in the midst of her;
she shall not be overthrown;
God shall help her at the break of day.
The nations make much ado, and the kingdoms are shaken;
God has spoken, and the earth shall melt away.
The Lord of hosts is with us;
the God of Jacob is our stronghold. *(Psalm 46:5-8 BCP)*

God is our refuge and strength,
a very present help in trouble.
Therefore we will not fear, though the earth be moved,
and though the mountains be toppled into the depths of the sea;
(Psalm 46:1-2 BCP)

The Lord's Prayer

And he said to me, "Son of man, have you seen this?"

Then he led me back to the bank of the river. As I went back, I saw
on the bank of the river very many trees on the one side and on the
other. And he said to me, "This water flows toward the eastern region
and goes down into the Arabah, and enters the sea; when the water
flows into the sea, the water will become fresh. And wherever the
river goes, every living creature that swarms will live, and there will
be very many fish. For this water goes there, that the waters of the
sea may become fresh; so everything will live where the river goes.
And on the banks, on both sides of the river, there will grow all kinds
of trees for food. Their leaves will not wither, nor their fruit fail, but
they will bear fresh fruit every month, because the water for them
flows from the sanctuary. Their fruit will be for food, and their leaves
for healing." *(Ezekiel 47:6-9, 12 ESV)*

O Lord, why do I let so much of this world come between me and you,
between me and your living water that can heal all that afflicts my heart,
mind, body, and soul? Heal me, O Lord! Lead me to your living water so
I may abide in you. Save me from this world and all its excuses, lies, and
doubts. Let me live fully in you, in your water where the leaves don't
wither and the fruit never fails to produce. Fill my heart with your light
and life, quenching my thirst with your living water. Amen.

Wednesday in the Fourth Week of Lent

"Very truly I tell you, whoever hears my word and believes him who sent me has eternal life and wil not be judged but has crossed over from death to life." (John 5:24 NIV)

Read: Isaiah 49:8–15, Psalm 145:8–19, John 5:19–29

Reflect:
- What does it mean to you to have eternal life in Christ?
- Are you living just for this world – or living for eternal life in Christ?
- How does it change your perspective to consider this life ju one small chapter in a much greater story?
- How is God sustaining you in your earthly wilderness, so th you endure to everlasting life in him?

Respond in Prayer:

✝ Shout for joy, you heavens;
  rejoice, you earth;
  burst into song, you mountains!
For the Lord comforts his people
  and will have compassion on his afflicted ones.

But Zion said, "The Lord has forsaken me,
  the Lord has forgotten me."

"Can a mother forget the baby at her breast
  and have no compassion on the child she has borne?
Though she may forget,
  I will not forget you! *(Isaiah 49:13-15 NIV)*

○ O Lord our God, you sustained your ancient people in the wildernes with bread from heaven: Feed now your pilgrim flock with the food that endures to everlasting life; through Jesus Christ your Son our Lord, who lives and reigns with you and the Holy Spirit, one God, for ever and ever. Amen. *(Collect for the Wednesday in the Fourth Week of Lent, BCP)*

∴ The eyes of all wait upon you, O Lord,
  and you give them their food in due season.
You open wide your hand
  and satisfy the needs of every living creature. *(Psalm 145:16-17 BCP)*

- Your kingdom is an everlasting kingdom;
  your dominion endures throughout all ages. *(Psalm 145:13 BCP)*

○ *The Lord's Prayer*

✝ So Jesus said to them, "Truly, truly, I say to you, the Son can do nothing of his own accord, but only what he sees the Father doing. For whatever the Father does, that the Son does likewise. For the Father loves the Son and shows him all that he himself is doing. And greater works than these will he show him, so that you may marvel. For as the Father raises the dead and gives them life, so also the Son gives life to whom he will. For the Father judges no one, but has given all judgment to the Son, that all may honor the Son, just as they honor the Father. Whoever does not honor the Son does not honor the Father who sent him. Truly, truly, I say to you, whoever hears my word and believes him who sent me has eternal life. He does not come into judgment, but has passed from death to life.

"Truly, truly, I say to you, an hour is coming, and is now here, when the dead will hear the voice of the Son of God, and those who hear will live. For as the Father has life in himself, so he has granted the Son also to have life in himself. And he has given him authority to execute judgment, because he is the Son of Man. Do not marvel at this, for an hour is coming when all who are in the tombs will hear his voice and come out, those who have done good to the resurrection of life, and those who have done evil to the resurrection of judgment. *(John 5:19-20 ESV)*

Almighty Father, I give thanks for all the ways in which you provide for my needs and sustain me through the desert seasons of my life. I give thanks for your love for me, never leaving me or forsaking me. Feed me with your bread of life, leading me to everlasting life in you. For this world is but a blink of an eye, a mere page in the book of my life. Sustain me through this earthly life, so that I may join your kingdom for all times. In your mercy, hear my prayer. Amen.

Thursday in the Fourth Week of Lent

"How can you believe since you accept glory from one another but do not seek the glory that comes from the only God?" (John 5:44 NIV)

Read: Exodus 32:7–14, Psalm 106:6–7,19–23, John 5:30–47

Reflect:

- How do you take notice and remember all that God is doing in your life? All that he has done in the lives of others and throughout Scripture?
- How can remembering God's glory and power help you stand firm in your faith?
- What glory are you seeking? The glory of God, or the glory of the world and others in your life?

Respond in Prayer:

✝ But Moses implored the Lord his God and said, "O Lord, why does your wrath burn hot against your people, whom you have brought out of the land of Egypt with great power and with a mighty hand? Why should the Egyptians say, 'With evil intent did he bring them out, to kill them in the mountains and to consume them from the face of the earth'? Turn from your burning anger and relent from this disaster against your people. Remember Abraham, Isaac, and Israel, your servants, to whom you swore by your own self, and said to them, 'I will multiply your offspring as the stars of heaven, and all this land that I have promised I will give to your offspring, and they shall inherit it forever.'" And the Lord relented from the disaster that he had spoken of bringing on his people. *(Exodus 32:11-14 ESV)*

○ Almighty and most merciful God, drive from us all weakness of body, mind, and spirit; that, being restored to wholeness, we may with free hearts become what you intend us to be and accomplish what you want us to do; through Jesus Christ our Lord, who lives and reigns with you and the Holy Spirit, one God, for ever and ever. Amen. *(Collect for the Thursday in the Fourth Week of Lent, BCP)*

⫶ Both we and our fathers have sinned;
we have committed iniquity; we have done wickedness.
Our fathers, when they were in Egypt,
did not consider your wondrous works;
they did not remember the abundance of your steadfast love,
but rebelled by the sea, at the Red Sea.
Yet he saved them for his name's sake,
that he might make known his mighty power. *(Psalm 106:6-8 ESV)*

● Save us, O Lord our God,
   and gather us from among the nations,
   that we may give thanks to your holy name
      and glory in your praise. *(Psalm 106:47 ESV)*

○ *The Lord's Prayer*

✝ By myself I can do nothing; I judge only as I hear, and my judgment is just, for I seek not to please myself but him who sent me.

"If I testify about myself, my testimony is not true. There is another who testifies in my favor, and I know that his testimony about me is true.

"You have sent to John and he has testified to the truth. Not that I accept human testimony; but I mention it that you may be saved. John was a lamp that burned and gave light, and you chose for a time to enjoy his light.

"I have testimony weightier than that of John. For the works that the Father has given me to finish—the very works that I am doing—testify that the Father has sent me. And the Father who sent me has himself testified concerning me. You have never heard his voice nor seen his form, nor does his word dwell in you, for you do not believe the one he sent. You study the Scriptures diligently because you think that in them you have eternal life. These are the very Scriptures that testify about me, yet you refuse to come to me to have life.

"I do not accept glory from human beings, but I know you. I know that you do not have the love of God in your hearts. I have come in my Father's name, and you do not accept me; but if someone else comes in his own name, you will accept him. How can you believe since you accept glory from one another but do not seek the glory that comes from the only God?

"But do not think I will accuse you before the Father. Your accuser is Moses, on whom your hopes are set. If you believed Moses, you would believe me, for he wrote about me. But since you do not believe what he wrote, how are you going to believe what I say?" *(John 5:30-47 NIV)*

O Lord, may I only ever seek your glory, and not the glory of this world. For the glory of this world is fleeting and thin, leading only to death and destruction. But, Lord, your glory is life and light. All who seek and live according to your glory will know you and have eternal life. Restore my heart to you, Lord, opening my eyes to see your glory all around, committing your glorious works to my memory for all time. May I never lose sight of you and your glory, Lord.

Friday in the Fourth Week of Lent

"Yes, you know me, and you know where I am from. I am not here on my own authority, but he who sent me is true. You do not know him, but I know him because I am from him and he sent me."
(John 7:28-29 NIV)

Read: Wisdom, 2:1a, 12-24, Psalm 34:15–22, John 7:1–2,10,25–30

Reflect:

- What do you believe about Jesus? Is he your Savior, the Messiah – or just a good man, a prophet?
- How do today's Scripture readings help you understand Jesus and know who he is?
- Are you still waiting for more proof about Jesus, or will you accept him at his word today and give him your heart?

Respond in Prayer:

They reasoned unsoundly, saying to themselves,
"Short and sorrowful is our life.

"Let us lie in wait for the righteous man,
because he is inconvenient to us and opposes our actions;
he reproaches us for sins against the law,
and accuses us of sins against our training.
He professes to have knowledge of God,
and calls himself a child of the Lord.
He became to us a reproof of our thoughts;
the very sight of him is a burden to us,
because his manner of life is unlike that of others,
and his ways are strange.
We are considered by him as something base,
and he avoids our ways as unclean;
he calls the last end of the righteous happy,
and boasts that God is his father.
Let us see if his words are true,
and let us test what will happen at the end of his life;
for if the righteous man is God's child, he will help him,
and will deliver him from the hand of his adversaries.
Let us test him with insult and torture,
so that we may find out how gentle he is,
and make trial of his forbearance.
Let us condemn him to a shameful death,
for, according to what he says, he will be protected."

Thus they reasoned, but they were led astray,
for their wickedness blinded them,
and they did not know the secret purposes of God,
nor hoped for the wages of holiness,
nor discerned the prize for blameless souls;
for God created us for incorruption,
and made us in the image of his own eternity,
but through the devil's envy death entered the world,
and those who belong to his company experience it.
(Wisdom, 2:1a, 12-24 NRSV)

○ O God, you have given us the Good News of your abounding love in your Son Jesus Christ: So fill our hearts with thankfulness that we may rejoice to proclaim the good tidings we have received; through Jesus Christ our Lord, who lives and reigns with you and the Holy Spirit, one God, for ever and ever. Amen. *(Collect for the Friday in the Fourth Week of Lent, BCP)*

⠶ The eyes of the Lord are on the righteous,
    and his ears are attentive to their cry;
but the face of the Lord is against those who do evil,
    to blot out their name from the earth. *(Psalm 34:15-16 NIV)*

● The Lord is close to the brokenhearted
    and saves those who are crushed in spirit. *(Psalm 34:18 NIV)*

○ *The Lord's Prayer*

☩ Some of the people of Jerusalem therefore said, "Is not this the man whom they seek to kill? And here he is, speaking openly, and they say nothing to him! Can it be that the authorities really know that this is the Christ? But we know where this man comes from, and when the Christ appears, no one will know where he comes from." So Jesus proclaimed, as he taught in the temple, "You know me, and you know where I come from. But I have not come of my own accord. He who sent me is true, and him you do not know. I know him, for I come from him, and he sent me." *(John 5:25-29 ESV)*

Lord, open my eyes to see you, open my heart to know you, open my ears to hear your teaching, open my soul to follow where you lead. For you are my Savior, the Messiah, the one sent from God to save us. Let me know these truths deep in my heart and proclaim your Good News to world. Amen.

Saturday in the Fourth Week of Lent

Jesus stood and said in a loud voice, "Let anyone who is thirsty come to me and drink. Whoever believes in me, as Scripture has said, rivers of living water will flow from within them."
(John 7:37-38 NIV)

Read: Jeremiah 11:18-20, Psalm 7:6-11, John 7:37-52

Reflect:

- As we've progressed through this season of Lent, have you fully acknowledged and confessed your sins to God?
- In what areas do you still need to humbly confess your sin and ask God for forgiveness? Will you do that today?
- Will you also join in prayer over everyone else who is coming before the Great Judge in humility to confess their sins and ask for God's loving mercy and forgiveness? Pray that all who come with repentant hearts will be forgiven. Pray for those too, who have not yet confessed, that they would yet come and kneel before God in repentance.

Respond in Prayer:

✝ But you, Lord Almighty, who judge righteously
and test the heart and mind,
let me see your vengeance on them,
for to you I have committed my cause. *(Jeremiah 11:20 ESV)*

○ Mercifully hear our prayers, O Lord, and spare all those who confess their sins to you; that those whose consciences are accused by sin may by your merciful pardon be absolved; through Jesus Christ your Son our Lord, who lives and reigns with you and the Holy Spirit, one God, for ever and ever. Amen. *(Collect for the Saturday in the Fourth Week of Lent BCP)*

⁘ Be seated on your lofty throne, O Most High;
O Lord, judge the nations.
Give judgment for me according to my righteousness, O Lord,
and according to my innocence, O Most High.
Let the malice of the wicked come to an end, but establish the righteous;
for you test the mind and heart, O righteous God. *(Psalm 7:8-10 BCP)*

● God is my shield and defense;
he is the savior of the true in heart. *(Psalm 7:11 BCP)*

The Lord's Prayer

On the last day of the feast, the great day, Jesus stood up and cried out, "If anyone thirsts, let him come to me and drink. Whoever believes in me, as the Scripture has said, 'Out of his heart will flow rivers of living water.'" Now this he said about the Spirit, whom those who believed in him were to receive, for as yet the Spirit had not been given, because Jesus was not yet glorified. When they heard these words, some of the people said, "This really is the Prophet." Others said, "This is the Christ." *(John 7:37-41 ESV)*

Holy Father, you sit in righteous judgement over us, allowing us to approach with humble and repentant hearts. Hear our prayers, O Lord, and wash us clean with your mercy and forgiveness. We pray for all the faithful who are coming before you to confess their sins, that you would search their hearts and know their souls, to restore the faithful to you. For you, Lord, are great and merciful, full of love for your children, even when we go astray. Forgive us and set us back on your way. Amen.

Monday in the Fifth Week of Lent

I am the light of the world. Whoever follows me will never walk in darkness, but will have the light of life." (John 8:12 NIV)

Read: Psalm 23, John 8:12-20

Reflect:
- What does it mean to you for Jesus to be the 'light of the world'?
- How is he the light of YOUR world?
- How does following Jesus bring light to the dark places of your life?

Respond in Prayer:

✝ When Jesus spoke again to the people, he said, "I am the light of the world. Whoever follows me will never walk in darkness, but will have the light of life."

The Pharisees challenged him, "Here you are, appearing as your own witness; your testimony is not valid."

Jesus answered, "Even if I testify on my own behalf, my testimony is valid, for I know where I came from and where I am going. But you have no idea where I come from or where I am going. You judge by human standards; I pass judgment on no one. But if I do judge, my decisions are true, because I am not alone. I stand with the Father, who sent me. In your own Law it is written that the testimony of two witnesses is true. I am one who testifies for myself; my other witness is the Father, who sent me."

Then they asked him, "Where is your father?"

"You do not know me or my Father," Jesus replied. "If you knew me, you would know my Father also." He spoke these words while teaching in the temple courts near the place where the offerings were put. Yet no one seized him, because his hour had not yet come. *(John 8:12-20 NIV)*

○ Be gracious to your people, we entreat you, O Lord, that they, repenting day by day of the things that displease you, may be more and more filled with love of you and of your commandments; and, being supported by your grace in this life, may come to the full enjoyment of eternal life in your everlasting kingdom; through Jesus Christ our Lord, who lives and reigns with you and the Holy Spirit, one God, for ever and ever. Amen. *(Collect for the Monday in the Fifth Week of Lent, BCP)*

Though I walk through the valley of the shadow of death, I shall fear no evil;

> for you are with me;
> your rod and your staff, they comfort me. *(Psalm 23:4 BCP)*

The Lord is my shepherd;

> I shall not be in want. *(Psalm 23:1 BCP)*

The Lord's Prayer

The Lord is my shepherd; I shall not want.

> He makes me lie down in green pastures.

He leads me beside still waters.

> He restores my soul.

He leads me in paths of righteousness

> for his name's sake.

Even though I walk through the valley of the shadow of death,

> I will fear no evil,

for you are with me;

> your rod and your staff,
> they comfort me.

You prepare a table before me

> in the presence of my enemies;

you anoint my head with oil;

> my cup overflows.

Surely goodness and mercy shall follow me

> all the days of my life,

and I shall dwell in the house of the Lord

> forever. *(Psalm 23 ESV)*

O Jesus, the light of this world, my shepherd and savior, I pray for your light to drive out all the darkness in my life. I pray for you to walk by my side through the valleys and dark seasons of my life, to fill me with your love and light. Pour out your grace upon me, one who isn't worthy of walking by your side, yet one who desires nothing more than to worship at your feet and walk in your light. Amen.

Tuesday in the Fifth Week of Lent

"You are from below; I am from above. You are of this world; I am not of this world."
(John 8:23 NIV)

Read: Numbers 21:4–9, Psalm 102:15–22, John 8:21–30

Reflect:

- Consider your earthly mortality compared with the eternity of Jesus. What does it mean to you when Jesus says he's not of this world?
- When you think of the briefness of this life on earth, what perspective does it give you for the eternal life we can have in Christ?
- What hope do we have in Christ that we will have eternal life when we believe and commit our lives to him?

Respond in Prayer:

Once more Jesus said to them, "I am going away, and you will look for me, and you will die in your sin. Where I go, you cannot come."

This made the Jews ask, "Will he kill himself? Is that why he says, 'Where I go, you cannot come'?"

But he continued, "You are from below; I am from above. You are of this world; I am not of this world. I told you that you would die in your sins; if you do not believe that I am he, you will indeed die in your sins."

"Who are you?" they asked.

"Just what I have been telling you from the beginning," Jesus replied. "I have much to say in judgment of you. But he who sent me is trustworthy, and what I have heard from him I tell the world."

They did not understand that he was telling them about his Father. Jesus said, "When you have lifted up the Son of Man, then you will know that I am he and that I do nothing on my own but speak just what the Father has taught me. The one who sent me is with me; he has not left me alone, for I always do what pleases him." Even as he spoke, many believed in him.

○ Almighty God, through the incarnate Word you have caused us to be born anew of an imperishable and eternal seed: Look with compassion upon those who are being prepared for Holy Baptism, and grant that they may be built as living stones into a spiritual temple acceptable to you; through Jesus Christ our Lord, who lives and reigns with you and the Holy Spirit, one God, for ever and ever. Amen. *(Collect for the Tuesday in the Fifth Week of Lent, BCP)*

Hear my prayer, O Lord;
    let my cry come to you!
Do not hide your face from me
    in the day of my distress!
Incline your ear to me;
    answer me speedily in the day when I call! *(Psalm 102:1-2 ESV)*

● My days are like an evening shadow;
    I wither away like grass.
But you, O Lord, are enthroned forever;
    you are remembered throughout all generations. *(Psalm 102:11-12 ESV)*

○ *The Lord's Prayer*

Of old you laid the foundation of the earth,
    and the heavens are the work of your hands.
They will perish, but you will remain;
    they will all wear out like a garment.
You will change them like a robe, and they will pass away,
    but you are the same, and your years have no end.
The children of your servants shall dwell secure;
    their offspring shall be established before you. *(Psalm 102:25-28 ESV)*

Heavenly and Almighty Father, the Alpha and the Omega, the One who is eternal and ever-living, have compassion on me, but a blink your eye, a speck of dust in your vast kingdom. For my life is but temporary and fleeting, but you are eternal. Lord, grant me eternal life in you. Let me be born afresh in you and live in your kingdom for ever. For you are the one to whom I want to give my life, to serve and honor you in this life and the next. Amen.

Wednesday in the Fifth Week of Lent

"If you abide in my word, you are truly my disciples, and you will know the truth, and the truth will . you free." (John 8:31-32 ESV)

Read: Daniel 3:14–20,24–28, John 8:31–42

Reflect:

- What does it mean to 'abide in Jesus' word'? How does tha look in your life?
- What difference did it mean to Shadrach, Meshach, and Abednego that they knew God and God's truth? How did t strength of their faith help them face their fiery trial?
- How will developing a stronger, deeper, more abiding faith help you face the fiery trials of your life?
- How will you commit to abiding deeper in Jesus and growir your faith beyond this Lenten season?

Respond in Prayer:

✝ Nebuchadnezzar answered and said to them, "Is it true, O Shadrach Meshach, and Abednego, that you do not serve my gods or worship the golden image that I have set up? Now if you are ready when you hear the sound of the horn, pipe, lyre, trigon, harp, bagpipe, and eve kind of music, to fall down and worship the image that I have made, well and good. But if you do not worship, you shall immediately be cast into a burning fiery furnace. And who is the god who will delive you out of my hands?"

Shadrach, Meshach, and Abednego answered and said to the king, "O Nebuchadnezzar, we have no need to answer you in this matter. If this be so, our God whom we serve is able to deliver us from the burning fiery furnace, and he will deliver us out of your hand, O kin; But if not, be it known to you, O king, that we will not serve your gods or worship the golden image that you have set up."

Then Nebuchadnezzar was filled with fury, and the expression of hi face was changed against Shadrach, Meshach, and Abednego. He ordered the furnace heated seven times more than it was usually heated. And he ordered some of the mighty men of his army to bin Shadrach, Meshach, and Abednego, and to cast them into the burni fiery furnace. *(Daniel 3:14-20 ESV)*

○ Almighty God our heavenly Father, renew in us the gifts of your mercy; increase our faith, strengthen our hope, enlighten our understanding, widen our charity, and make us ready to serve you; through Jesus Christ our Lord, who lives and reigns with you and the Holy Spirit, one God, for ever and ever. Amen. *(Collect for the Wednesday in the Fifth Week of Lent, BCP)*

∴ Glory to you, Father, Son, and Holy Spirit;
I will praise you and highly exalt you for ever. *(Canticle 13, BCP)*

● Jesus, If I abide in your word, I will truly be your disciple, and I will know the truth, and the truth will set me free. *(John 8:31-32, ESV)*

○ *The Lord's Prayer*

✠ Glory to you, Lord God of our fathers;
   you are worthy of praise; glory to you.
Glory to you for the radiance of your holy Name;
   we will praise you and highly exalt you for ever.
Glory to you in the splendor of your temple;
   on the throne of your majesty, glory to you.
Glory to you, seated between the Cherubim;
   we will praise you and highly exalt you for ever.
Glory to you, beholding the depths;
   in the high vault of heaven, glory to you.
Glory to you, Father, Son, and Holy Spirit;
   we will praise you and highly exalt you for ever. *(Canticle 13, BCP)*

O Jesus, let me abide in you and in your word, to know your truth and truly be set free. Open my eyes to see and my ears to hear. May I know you and be set free from all that shackles and binds in this earthly world. For living according to this world leads only to sin and death, but living and abiding in you lead to light and life. Lord, help me develop the depth of faith and understanding to put all my trust and hope in you, with a faith able to withstand any of the trials and storms of this earth. For you are the truth and the light, the one I want to follow with all my heart. Amen.

Thursday in the Fifth Week of Lent

"Very truly I tell you, whoever obeys my word will never see death."
(John 8:51 NIV)

Read: Genesis 17:1–8, Psalm 105:4–11, John 8:51–59

Reflect:

- Consider the connection between Abraham and Jesus. Hear Jesus say, "Truly, truly, I say to you, before Abraham was, I am."
- How does that affect what you know of God, Jesus, and the Holy Spirit? How does it impact your understanding of Jesus to consider that he didn't just come into existence for his ministry on earth, but has been since the beginning of time.
- How does Jesus explaining his relationship with Abraham help you understand Jesus' promise that if we obey his word we will never see death? Jesus came before Abraham, knew Abraham, and Abraham in heaven greatly rejoiced in Jesus coming to save us.

Respond in Prayer:

✝ When Abram was ninety-nine years old, the Lord appeared to him and said, "I am God Almighty; walk before me faithfully and be blameless. Then I will make my covenant between me and you and will greatly increase your numbers."

Abram fell facedown, and God said to him, "As for me, this is my covenant with you: You will be the father of many nations. No longer will you be called Abram; your name will be Abraham, for I have made you a father of many nations. I will make you very fruitful; I will make nations of you, and kings will come from you. I will establish my covenant as an everlasting covenant between me and you and your descendants after you for the generations to come, to be your God and the God of your descendants after you. The whole land of Canaan, where you now reside as a foreigner, I will give as an everlasting possession to you and your descendants after you; and I will be their God." *(Genesis 17:1-8 NIV)*

○ O God, you have called us to be your children, and have promised that those who suffer with Christ will be heirs with him of your glory: Arm us with such trust in him that we may ask no rest from his demands and have no fear in his service; through Jesus Christ our Lord, who lives and reigns with you and the Holy Spirit, one God, for ever and ever. Amen. *(Collect for the Thursday in the Fifth Week of Lent, BCP)*

Remember the wonders he has done,
   his miracles, and the judgments he pronounced,
you his servants, the descendants of Abraham,
   his chosen ones, the children of Jacob.
He is the Lord our God;
   his judgments are in all the earth.
He remembers his covenant forever,
   the promise he made, for a thousand generations *(Psalm 105:5-8 NIV)*

● I will look to the Lord and his strength;
   I will seek his face always. *(Psalm 105:4 NIV)*

○ *The Lord's Prayer*

✝ Truly, truly, I say to you, if anyone keeps my word, he will never see death." The Jews said to him, "Now we know that you have a demon! Abraham died, as did the prophets, yet you say, 'If anyone keeps my word, he will never taste death.' Are you greater than our father Abraham, who died? And the prophets died! Who do you make yourself out to be?" Jesus answered, "If I glorify myself, my glory is nothing. It is my Father who glorifies me, of whom you say, 'He is our God.' But you have not known him. I know him. If I were to say that I do not know him, I would be a liar like you, but I do know him and I keep his word. Your father Abraham rejoiced that he would see my day. He saw it and was glad." So the Jews said to him, "You are not yet fifty years old, and have you seen Abraham?" Jesus said to them, "Truly, truly, I say to you, before Abraham was, I am." So they picked up stones to throw at him, but Jesus hid himself and went out of the temple. *(John 8:51-59 ESV)*

Heavenly and Almighty Father, the Great I AM, the beginning and the end, let me place my trust in you. Help me follow your rule and trust in your way, leading me to everlasting life in you. For your rule is love and your will for us to bring you glory. You want only good things for your children, if we'll only trust in your and follow where you lead. I will look to you always and see your strength, abiding and trusting you alone. For you are good and holy and just. Amen.

Friday in the Fifth Week of Lent

"They said, "Though John never performed a sign, all that John said about this man was true." And that place many believed in Jesus." (John 10:41-42 NIV)

Read: Jeremiah 20:7-13, Psalm 18:1-7. John 10:31-42

Reflect:

- Consider this statement from Jesus: "even though you do not believe me, believe the works, that you may know and understand that the Father is in me and I am in the Father."
- How do the works Jesus did help you believe in him and understand he is God's Son?
- In the same passage from John, people commented that everything John said about Jesus was true and many people decided that day to believe in Jesus. How have you seen through the Scripture that everything said about Jesus is true – from Genesis to Revelations? How does that help you believe in Jesus?
- Will you accept Jesus for all he is, committing to follow him with a joyful and obedient heart?

Respond in Prayer:

But the Lord is with me like a mighty warrior;
    so my persecutors will stumble and not prevail.
They will fail and be thoroughly disgraced;
    their dishonor will never be forgotten.
Lord Almighty, you who examine the righteous
    and probe the heart and mind,
let me see your vengeance on them,
    for to you I have committed my cause.
Sing to the Lord!
    Give praise to the Lord!
He rescues the life of the needy
    from the hands of the wicked. *(Jeremiah 20:11-13 NIV)*

O Lord, you relieve our necessity out of the abundance of your great riches: Grant that we may accept with joy the salvation you bestow, and manifest it to all the world by the quality of our lives; through Jesus Christ our Lord, who lives and reigns with you and the Holy Spirit, one God, now and for ever. Amen. *(Collect for the Friday in the Fifth Week of Lent, BCP)*

I called upon the Lord in my distress
   and cried out to my God for help.
He heard my voice from his heavenly dwelling;
   my cry of anguish came to his ears. *(Psalm 18:6-7 BCP)*

My God, my rock in whom I put my trust,
   my shield, the horn of my salvation, and my refuge;
   you are worthy of praise. *(Psalm 18:2 BCP)*

The Lord's Prayer

The Jews picked up stones again to stone him. Jesus answered them, "I have shown you many good works from the Father; for which of them are you going to stone me?" The Jews answered him, "It is not for a good work that we are going to stone you but for blasphemy, because you, being a man, make yourself God." Jesus answered them, "Is it not written in your Law, 'I said, you are gods'? If he called them gods to whom the word of God came—and Scripture cannot be broken— do you say of him whom the Father consecrated and sent into the world, 'You are blaspheming,' because I said, 'I am the Son of God'? If I am not doing the works of my Father, then do not believe me; but if I do them, even though you do not believe me, believe the works, that you may know and understand that the Father is in me and I am in the Father." Again they sought to arrest him, but he escaped from their hands.

He went away again across the Jordan to the place where John had been baptizing at first, and there he remained. And many came to him. And they said, "John did no sign, but everything that John said about this man was true." And many believed in him there. *(John 10:31-42 ESV)*

Jesus, you are enough for me. As I search the Scriptures and search my own understanding, I see that everything said about you is true. You truly are of God and are God's Son. You are the Good Shepherd, Mighty Counselor, Bread of Life, Son of the Most High, Immanuel, King of Kings, the Truth, the Way, and the Life Everlasting, and My Redeemer and Savior. To you I give my heart, to walk in your way with joy and obedience. Lord, lead me. Amen.

Saturday in the Fifth Week of Lent

"For I will save them from all their sinful backsliding, and I will cleanse them. They will be my people, and I will be their God." (Ezekiel 37:23 NIV)

Read: Ezekiel 37:21–28, Psalm 85:1–7, John 11:45–53

Reflect:

- As you've reflected over your own sinful 'backsliding' this Lenten season, where do you still need to work with God to confess and repent?
- God desires to wash you clean and restore you to him, so will you confess your sins, repent and ask God's help to turn from those sins?

Respond in Prayer:

✟ Therefore many of the Jews who had come to visit Mary, and had seen what Jesus did, believed in him. But some of them went to the Pharisees and told them what Jesus had done. Then the chief priests and the Pharisees called a meeting of the Sanhedrin.

"What are we accomplishing?" they asked. "Here is this man performing many signs. If we let him go on like this, everyone will believe in him, and then the Romans will come and take away both our temple and our nation."

Then one of them, named Caiaphas, who was high priest that year, spoke up, "You know nothing at all! You do not realize that it is better for you that one man die for the people than that the whole nation perish."

He did not say this on his own, but as high priest that year he prophesied that Jesus would die for the Jewish nation, and not only for that nation but also for the scattered children of God, to bring them together and make them one. So from that day on they plotted to take his life. *(John 11:45-53 NIV)*

○ O Lord, in your goodness you bestow abundant graces on your elect. Look with favor, we entreat you, upon those who in these Lenten days are being prepared for Holy Baptism, and grant them the help of your protection; through Jesus Christ your Son our Lord, who lives and reigns with you and the Holy Spirit, one God, for ever and ever. Amen. *(Collect for the Saturday in the Fifth Week of Lent, BCP)*

∴ You have been gracious to your land, O Lord,
  you have restored the good fortune of Jacob.
You have forgiven the iniquity of your people
  and blotted out all their sins.
You have withdrawn all your fury
  and turned yourself from your wrathful indignation.
Restore us then, O God our Savior. *(Psalm 85:1-4 BCP)*

● Show me your mercy, O Lord,
and grant me your salvation. *(Psalm 85:7 BCP)*

○ *The Lord's Prayer*

☦ Then say to them, Thus says the Lord God: Behold, I will take the people of Israel from the nations among which they have gone, and will gather them from all around, and bring them to their own land. And I will make them one nation in the land, on the mountains of Israel. And one king shall be king over them all, and they shall be no longer two nations, and no longer divided into two kingdoms. They shall not defile themselves anymore with their idols and their detestable things, or with any of their transgressions. But I will save them from all the backslidings in which they have sinned, and will cleanse them; and they shall be my people, and I will be their God.

"My servant David shall be king over them, and they shall all have one shepherd. They shall walk in my rules and be careful to obey my statutes. They shall dwell in the land that I gave to my servant Jacob, where your fathers lived. They and their children and their children's children shall dwell there forever, and David my servant shall be their prince forever. I will make a covenant of peace with them. It shall be an everlasting covenant with them. And I will set them in their land and multiply them, and will set my sanctuary in their midst forevermore. My dwelling place shall be with them, and I will be their God, and they shall be my people. Then the nations will know that I am the Lord who sanctifies Israel, when my sanctuary is in their midst forevermore." *(Ezekiel 37:21-28 ESV)*

Heavenly Father, cleanse me of all my sinful backsliding and transgressions, for I am a mere mortal, broken and sinful. Yet, you are gracious and merciful, ready to hear my confession and cleanse me of my wrongdoings. Lord, forgive me for these sins and help me make the changes you desire in my life. Lead me on better paths, toward wiser choices, choosing love over all to shine your light in this world. Show me your mercy, O Lord, and grant me your salvation. Amen.

Monday in Holy Week

"How much more, then, will the blood of Christ, who through the eternal Spirit offered himself unblemished to God, cleanse our consciences from acts that lead to death, so that we may serve the living God!" (Hebrews 9:15 NIV)

Read: Isaiah 42:1-9, Psalm 36:5-11, Hebrews 9:11-15, John 12:1-11

Reflect:

- How does walking in the way of the cross lead to light and life? What does God promise us about following Jesus?
- As we begin this final week of Lent, this Holy Week leading to Easter, how can you submit yourself to walk in the way of the cross, placing your hope and trust in Jesus?
- Take time to read the Gospel readings this week and step fully into the story with Jesus and the disciples. Deeply feel the emotions of the week, so you can more vividly experience the joy of Easter on Sunday.

Respond in Prayer:

✝ This is what God the Lord says—
the Creator of the heavens, who stretches them out,
who spreads out the earth with all that springs from it,
who gives breath to its people,
and life to those who walk on it:
"I, the Lord, have called you in righteousness;
I will take hold of your hand.
I will keep you and will make you
to be a covenant for the people
and a light for the Gentiles,
to open eyes that are blind,
to free captives from prison
and to release from the dungeon those who sit in darkness.
"I am the Lord; that is my name!
I will not yield my glory to another
or my praise to idols.
See, the former things have taken place,
and new things I declare;
before they spring into being
I announce them to you." *(Isaiah 42:5-9 NIV)*

○ Almighty God, whose most dear Son went not up to joy but first he suffered pain, and entered not into glory before he was crucified: Mercifully grant that we, walking in the way of the cross, may find it none other than the way of life and peace; through Jesus Christ your Son our Lord, who lives and reigns with you and the Holy Spirit, one God, for ever and ever. Amen. *(Collect for the Monday in Holy Week, BCP)*

Your love, O Lord, reaches to the heavens,
   and your faithfulness to the clouds.
Your righteousness is like the strong mountains,
    your justice like the great deep;
    you save both man and beast, O Lord.
How priceless is your love, O God!
    your people take refuge under the shadow of your wings. *(Psalm 36:5-7 BCP)*

● For with you is the well of life,
    and in your light we see light. *(Psalm 36:9 BCP)*

○ *The Lord's Prayer*

But when Christ appeared as a high priest of the good things that have come, then through the greater and more perfect tent (not made with hands, that is, not of this creation) he entered once for all into the holy places, not by means of the blood of goats and calves but by means of his own blood, thus securing an eternal redemption. For if the blood of goats and bulls, and the sprinkling of defiled persons with the ashes of a heifer, sanctify for the purification of the flesh, how much more will the blood of Christ, who through the eternal Spirit offered himself without blemish to God, purify our conscience from dead works to serve the living God.

Therefore he is the mediator of a new covenant, so that those who are called may receive the promised eternal inheritance, since a death has occurred that redeems them from the transgressions committed under the first covenant. *(Hebrews 9:11-15 ESV)*

Almighty Father, who sent your only Son Jesus Christ to save us from our sin, show me how I can honor you and bring glory to your name, by walking in the way of Jesus. Give me grace and mercy as I try and fail, guidance when I'm not sure which way to go, and wisdom to trust you in all things. For your love brings light and life to all who seek it. May I seek you ever more as I walk with you through this Holy Week and beyond. Amen.

Tuesday in Holy Week

"Anyone who loves their life will lose it, while anyone who hates their life in this world will keep it f eternal life. Whoever serves me must follow me; and where I am, my servant also will be. My Fath will honor the one who serves me." (John 12:25-26 NIV)

Read: Isaiah 49:1-7, Psalm 71:1-14, 1 Corinthians 1:18-31, John 12:20-3€

Reflect:

- God chose the foolish, the weak, and the low to serve his glory. He didn't come in a great show of power and might, but in humility. Jesus died on a cross, a most humiliating ar painful death. These were great stumbling blocks to many i recognizing who Jesus was and believing. What about you?
- Jesus said, "if anyone serves me, he must follow me." How are you picking up your cross and following him?
- Jesus said "do not let darkness overtake you... become children of the light". How are you putting your trust in Jesu to save and protect you from the darkness of this life? How will you commit your heart to him and walk in his light?

Respond in Prayer:

✝ And Jesus answered them, "The hour has come for the Son of Man be glorified. Truly, truly, I say to you, unless a grain of wheat falls int the earth and dies, it remains alone; but if it dies, it bears much frui Whoever loves his life loses it, and whoever hates his life in this wo will keep it for eternal life. If anyone serves me, he must follow me; and where I am, there will my servant be also. If anyone serves me, the Father will honor him.

"Now is my soul troubled. And what shall I say? 'Father, save me fro this hour'? But for this purpose I have come to this hour. Father, glorify your name." Then a voice came from heaven: "I have glorifiec it, and I will glorify it again." The crowd that stood there and heard it said that it had thundered. Others said, "An angel has spoken to him." Jesus answered, "This voice has come for your sake, not mine. Now is the judgment of this world; now will the ruler of this world be cast out. And I, when I am lifted up from the earth, will draw all people to myself." He said this to show by what kind of death he wε going to die. So the crowd answered him, "We have heard from the Law that the Christ remains forever. How can you say that the Son of Man must be lifted up? Who is this Son of Man?" So Jesus said tc them, "The light is among you for a little while longer. Walk while yc have the light, lest darkness overtake you. The one who walks in the darkness does not know where he is going. While you have the ligh believe in the light, that you may become sons of light." *(John 12:23-3€ ESV)*

O God, by the passion of your blessed Son you made an instrument of shameful death to be for us the means of life: Grant us so to glory in the cross of Christ, that we may gladly suffer shame and loss for the sake of your Son our Savior Jesus Christ; who lives and reigns with you and the Holy Spirit, one God, for ever and ever. Amen. *(Collect for the Tuesday in Holy Week, BCP)*

In you, Lord, I have taken refuge;
    let me never be put to shame.
In your righteousness, rescue me and deliver me;
    turn your ear to me and save me.
As for me, I will always have hope;
    I will praise you more and more. *(Psalm 71:1-2,14 NIV)*

Be my rock of refuge,
    to which I can always go;
give the command to save me,
    for you are my rock and my fortress. *(Psalm 71:3 NIV)*

The Lord's Prayer

For the message of the cross is foolishness to those who are perishing, but to us who are being saved it is the power of God. For it is written:

"I will destroy the wisdom of the wise;
    the intelligence of the intelligent I will frustrate."

Brothers and sisters, think of what you were when you were called. Not many of you were wise by human standards; not many were influential; not many were of noble birth. But God chose the foolish things of the world to shame the wise; God chose the weak things of the world to shame the strong. God chose the lowly things of this world and the despised things—and the things that are not—to nullify the things that are, so that no one may boast before him. It is because of him that you are in Christ Jesus, who has become for us wisdom from God—that is, our righteousness, holiness and redemption. Therefore, as it is written: "Let the one who boasts boast in the Lord." *(1 Corinthians 1:18-19, 26-31 NIV)*

O Heavenly and Almighty Father, who sent his only Son Jesus to live and die as one of us, save me. For all wisdom, all strength, and all glory is in you. You are my rock and my redeemer, my shelter in the storm. In you I place my trust, so that I may have hope. Let me walk in your light all my days, seeking only you. I give you my life to love and serve you, following you in all that I do. Amen.

Wednesday in Holy Week

"Therefore, since we are surrounded by such a great cloud of witnesses, let us throw off everything that hinders and the sin that so easily entangles. And let us run with perseverance the race marked out for us, fixing our eyes on Jesus." (Hebrews 12:1-2 NIV)

Read: Isaiah 50:4-9a, Psalm 70, Hebrews 12:1-3, John 13:21-32

Reflect:

- Jesus endured rejection, shame, betrayal, persecution, and more. We are not promised an easy road as believers. In fact we're promised that a life of following Christ will be difficult. So, how can you persevere in your journey to follow Jesus?
- How can you take hope and encouragement from the "great cloud of witnesses" to endure the race before you, with joy?
- How can you 'throw off everything that hinders and the sin that so easily entangles", so you can step fully into the life God has planned for you?

Respond in Prayer:

After he had said this, Jesus was troubled in spirit and testified, "Very truly I tell you, one of you is going to betray me."

His disciples stared at one another, at a loss to know which of them he meant. One of them, the disciple whom Jesus loved, was reclining next to him. Simon Peter motioned to this disciple and said, "Ask him which one he means."

Leaning back against Jesus, he asked him, "Lord, who is it?"

Jesus answered, "It is the one to whom I will give this piece of bread when I have dipped it in the dish." Then, dipping the piece of bread, he gave it to Judas, the son of Simon Iscariot. As soon as Judas took the bread, Satan entered into him.

So Jesus told him, "What you are about to do, do quickly." But no one at the meal understood why Jesus said this to him. Since Judas had charge of the money, some thought Jesus was telling him to buy what was needed for the festival, or to give something to the poor. As soon as Judas had taken the bread, he went out. And it was night.

When he was gone, Jesus said, "Now the Son of Man is glorified and God is glorified in him. If God is glorified in him, God will glorify the Son in himself, and will glorify him at once. *(John 13:21-32 NIV)*

○ Lord God, whose blessed Son our Savior gave his body to be whipped and his face to be spit upon: Give us grace to accept joyfully the sufferings of the present time, confident of the glory that shall be revealed; through Jesus Christ your Son our Lord, who lives and reigns with you and the Holy Spirit, one God, for ever and ever. Amen. *(Collect for the Wednesday in Holy Week, BCP)*

But as for me, I am poor and needy;
   come to me speedily, O God.
You are my helper and my deliverer;
   O Lord, do not tarry. *(Psalm 70:5-6 BCP)*

● Let all who seek you rejoice and be glad in you;
   let those who love your salvation say for ever,
   "Great is the Lord!" *(Psalm 70:4 BCP)*

○ *The Lord's Prayer*

✠ Therefore, since we are surrounded by so great a cloud of witnesses, let us also lay aside every weight, and sin which clings so closely, and let us run with endurance the race that is set before us, looking to Jesus, the founder and perfecter of our faith, who for the joy that was set before him endured the cross, despising the shame, and is seated at the right hand of the throne of God.

Consider him who endured from sinners such hostility against himself, so that you may not grow weary or fainthearted. *(Hebrews 12:1-3 ESV)*

Jesus, you suffered greatly for our benefit. You walked the hard road through shame, betrayal, persecution, rejection. Yet, you only desired good things for us. You came in glory to save us and redeem us from our sins. You came to offer us light and life, a hope in you that surpasses anything the world can offer. So, why do we too often turn our backs? Why do we give in to questions and disbelief when the road gets hard? Why do we look for easier paths to follow? Lord, lead me in your way, encouraging me to persevere on the hard days, remembering the great hope I have in you. Amen.

Maundy Thursday

"A new command I give you: Love one another. As I have loved you, so you must love one another. By this everyone will know that you are my disciples, if you love one another." (John 13:34-35 NIV)

Read: Exodus 12:1-14, Psalm 116:1, 10-17, 1 Corinthians 11:23-26
John 13:1-17, 31b-35

Reflect:

- How are you living out Jesus' commandment to love one another as he loves you? Are there areas of your life where you need to bring this into more focus?
- Jesus humbled himself to wash the feet of his disciples, explaining that to lead you must serve. How are you leading – in your family, in your work, in your church, in your community? Are you leading by serving? How can you be a better leader by following Jesus' example?

Respond in Prayer:

✠ Now before the Feast of the Passover, when Jesus knew that his hour had come to depart out of this world to the Father, having loved his own who were in the world, he loved them to the end. During supper, when the devil had already put it into the heart of Judas Iscariot, Simon's son, to betray him, Jesus, knowing that the Father had given all things into his hands, and that he had come from God and was going back to God, rose from supper. He laid aside his outer garments, and taking a towel, tied it around his waist. Then he poured water into a basin and began to wash the disciples' feet and to wipe them with the towel that was wrapped around him. He came to Simon Peter, who said to him, "Lord, do you wash my feet?" Jesus answered him, "What I am doing you do not understand now, but afterward you will understand." Peter said to him, "You shall never wash my feet." Jesus answered him, "If I do not wash you, you have no share with me." Simon Peter said to him, "Lord, not my feet only but also my hands and my head!" Jesus said to him, "The one who has bathed does not need to wash, except for his feet, but is completely clean. And you are clean, but not every one of you." For he knew who was to betray him; that was why he said, "Not all of you are clean."

When he had washed their feet and put on his outer garments and resumed his place, he said to them, "Do you understand what I have done to you? You call me Teacher and Lord, and you are right, for so I am. If I then, your Lord and Teacher, have washed your feet, you also ought to wash one another's feet.

For I have given you an example, that you also should do just as I have done to you. Truly, truly, I say to you, a servant is not greater than his master, nor is a messenger greater than the one who sent him. If you know these things, blessed are you if you do them. *(John 13:1-17 ESV)*

Almighty Father, whose dear Son, on the night before he suffered, instituted the Sacrament of his Body and Blood: Mercifully grant that we may receive it thankfully in remembrance of Jesus Christ our Lord, who in these holy mysteries gives us a pledge of eternal life; and who now lives and reigns with you and the Holy Spirit, one God, for ever and ever. Amen. *(Collect for Maundy Thursday, BCP)*

I love the Lord, because he has heard the voice of my supplication,
  because he has inclined his ear to me whenever I called upon him.
How shall I repay the Lord
  for all the good things he has done for me? *(Psalm 116:1,10 BCP)*

I will lift up the cup of salvation
  and call upon the Name of the Lord.
I will fulfill my vows to the Lord
  in the presence of all his people. *(Psalm 116:11-12 BCP)*

The Lord's Prayer

When he was gone, Jesus said, "Now the Son of Man is glorified and God is glorified in him. If God is glorified in him,[God will glorify the Son in himself, and will glorify him at once.

"My children, I will be with you only a little longer. You will look for me, and just as I told the Jews, so I tell you now: Where I am going, you cannot come.

"A new command I give you: Love one another. As I have loved you, so you must love one another. By this everyone will know that you are my disciples, if you love one another." *(John 13:31-35 NIV)*

O Lord, the King of Kings, who led and taught not as a mighty ruler, but a servant leader, show me how to lead and live through love. Teach me how to love and serve others with a gracious and humble heart. Help me to always remember your words, being reminded each time I come before your table to share in the cup and the bread. As I come before you to eat the bread of redemption and drink the cup of your salvation, may I recommit my heart to serving you and leading through love. To you, O Lord, who are mighty to save, pour out your mercy and grace and lead me in your way. Amen.

Good Friday

"Son though he was, he learned obedience from what he suffered and, once made perfect, he beca
the source of eternal salvation for all who obey him" (Hebrews 5:8-9 NIV)

Read: Isaiah 52:13-53:12, Psalm 22, Hebrews 4:14-16, 5:7-9,
John 18:1-19:42

Reflect:
- Spend time today walking the road to Golgotha with Christ
  Read today's Gospel reading, imagining you are there
  witnessing Jesus' final day and his death. Sit with those
  emotions, the grief, the emptiness of a world with Christ.
- Consider a world without Christ. How does this make you
  feel? What would be missing from your life without Jesus?
- What must have his followers thought as he died, not
  knowing what the next days would bring? How would you
  have reacted?
- Knowing the rest of the story, how can you find hope in
  Good Friday?

Respond in Prayer:

✝ He was despised and rejected by mankind,
   a man of suffering, and familiar with pain.
Like one from whom people hide their faces
   he was despised, and we held him in low esteem.
Yet it was the Lord's will to crush him and cause him to suffer,
   and though the Lord makes his life an offering for sin,
he will see his offspring and prolong his days,
   and the will of the Lord will prosper in his hand.
After he has suffered,
   he will see the light of life and be satisfied;
by his knowledge my righteous servant will justify many,
   and he will bear their iniquities.
Therefore I will give him a portion among the great,
   and he will divide the spoils with the strong,
because he poured out his life unto death,
   and was numbered with the transgressors.
For he bore the sin of many,
   and made intercession for the transgressors. *(Isaiah 53:3, 10-12 NIV)*

○ Almighty God, we pray you graciously to behold this your family, fo
   whom our Lord Jesus Christ was willing to be betrayed, and given ir
   the hands of sinners, and to suffer death upon the cross; who now
   lives and reigns with you and the Holy Spirit, one God, for ever and
   ever. Amen. *(Collect for Good Friday, BCP)*

My God, my God, why have you forsaken me?
  and are so far from my cry
  and from the words of my distress?
O my God, I cry in the daytime, but you do not answer;
  by night as well, but I find no rest.
Yet you are the Holy One,
  enthroned upon the praises of Israel.
Our forefathers put their trust in you;
  they trusted, and you delivered them. *(Psalm 22:1-4 BCP)*

Be not far away, O Lord;
  you are my strength; hasten to help me.
I will declare your Name to my brethren;
  in the midst of the congregation I will praise you. *(Psalm 22:18, 21 BCP)*

The Lord's Prayer

Since then we have a great high priest who has passed through the heavens, Jesus, the Son of God, let us hold fast our confession. For we do not have a high priest who is unable to sympathize with our weaknesses, but one who in every respect has been tempted as we are, yet without sin. Let us then with confidence draw near to the throne of grace, that we may receive mercy and find grace to help in time of need.

In the days of his flesh, Jesus offered up prayers and supplications, with loud cries and tears, to him who was able to save him from death, and he was heard because of his reverence. Although he was a son, he learned obedience through what he suffered. And being made perfect, he became the source of eternal salvation to all who obey him. *(Hebrews 4:14-16; 5:7-9 ESV)*

O Jesus, on this day we remember your death, the day your light went out from this earth. We sit in the darkness today, remembering the trials you faced on our behalf. You have borne our sin and made the ultimate sacrifice to save us. Today, as we recall your final hours, we consider a world without you and hold onto the hope we know we have in you. Lord, commit my heart ever closer to you, because I don't want to live in a Good Friday world without you. I want you and your light in my life. I believe in you and want to follow you all the days of my life, even knowing the road ahead will be difficult. Come, Lord Jesus, come and fill this world with your light. Amen.

Holy Saturday

"The end of all things is near. Therefore be alert and of sober mind so that you may pray. Above a[ ] love each other deeply, because love covers over a multitude of sins." (1 Peter 4:7-8 NIV)

Read: Lamentations 3:1-9, 19-24, Psalm 31:1-4, 15-16
1 Peter 4:1-8, Matthew 27:57-66

Reflect:

- As you observe Holy Saturday, the day we hold vigil while Jesus lay in the tomb, consider the depths of God's love fo[ ] you by giving his own Son to save you.
- Knowing what comes tomorrow in the story, how does tod[ ] help you better trust in God? Could the disciples have fully envision the next chapters in Jesus' story? How do you think they still trusted in God, even through these latest events?
- How can you trust in God, even when his ways don't seem [ ] make sense and the days are dark? How can you still trust God's love for you?

Respond in Prayer:

✝ As evening approached, there came a rich man from Arimathea, named Joseph, who had himself become a disciple of Jesus. Going [ ] Pilate, he asked for Jesus' body, and Pilate ordered that it be given to him. Joseph took the body, wrapped it in a clean linen cloth, and placed it in his own new tomb that he had cut out of the rock. He rolled a big stone in front of the entrance to the tomb and went aw[ ] Mary Magdalene and the other Mary were sitting there opposite th[ ] tomb.

The next day, the one after Preparation Day, the chief priests and t[ ] Pharisees went to Pilate. "Sir," they said, "we remember that while he was still alive that deceiver said, 'After three days I will rise again[ ] So give the order for the tomb to be made secure until the third da[ ] Otherwise, his disciples may come and steal the body and tell the people that he has been raised from the dead. This last deception w[ ] be worse than the first."

"Take a guard," Pilate answered. "Go, make the tomb as secure as yo[ ] know how." So they went and made the tomb secure by putting a se[ ] on the stone and posting the guard. *(Matthew 27:57-66 NIV)*

○ O God, Creator of heaven and earth: Grant that, as the crucified body of your dear Son was laid in the tomb and rested on this holy Sabbath, so we may await with him the coming of the third day, and rise with him to newness of life; who now lives and reigns with you and the Holy Spirit, one God, for ever and ever. Amen. *(Collect for Holy Saturday, BCP)*

∴ In you, O Lord, have I taken refuge;
      let me never be put to shame;
      deliver me in your righteousness.
  Incline your ear to me;
      make haste to deliver me.
  Be my strong rock, a castle to keep me safe,
      for you are my crag and my stronghold;
      for the sake of your Name, lead me and guide me. *(Psalm 31:1-3 BCP)*

● The steadfast love of the Lord never ceases;
      his mercies never come to an end;
  they are new every morning;
      great is your faithfulness.
  "The Lord is my portion," says my soul,
      "therefore I will hope in him." *(Lamentations 3:22-24 ESV)*

○ *The Lord's Prayer*

☦ Since therefore Christ suffered in the flesh, arm yourselves with the same way of thinking, for whoever has suffered in the flesh has ceased from sin, so as to live for the rest of the time in the flesh no longer for human passions but for the will of God.

The end of all things is at hand; therefore be self-controlled and sober-minded for the sake of your prayers. Above all, keep loving one another earnestly, since love covers a multitude of sins.
(1 Peter 4:1-2, 7-8 ESV)

Heavenly Father, what great love you have for me that you would send your only begotten Son to die for my sins. How can I ever doubt your love or your ways? Yet in these dark moments, I start to question and doubt. I wonder what comes next and I fail to recall your great faithfulness. Lord, forgive my unbelief and help me believe. Help me to trust you in all things, in all times, even through the valleys and dark seasons of my life. For you are my rock and my refuge, my strength in the storm. Your love never ceases, your mercies never end. You are enough for me – more than enough. Help to me to remember that all the days of my life. Lead me to walk in love, as a shining reflection of your love into this world. And help me live the life you desire of me, bringing glory to you in all that I do. Amen.

Feast of St. Joseph

"Therefore, the promise comes by faith, so that it may be by grace and may be guaranteed to all Abraham's offspring." (Romans 4:16 NIV)

The Feast of St. Joseph is celebrated each year on March 19th, as a celebration of Joseph, the husband of Mary and step-father of Jesus. This day is celebrated in many countries, typically with foods considered 'lucky', such as fava beans (which were the only foods to survive a drought in the Middle Ages in Italy), lemons and foods containing sawdust/breadcrumbs, since Joseph was a carpenter. The table may also include fish and seafood, since St. Joseph's Day falls during Lent when meat is not traditionally served.

Read: 2 Samuel 7:4,8-16, Psalm 89:1-4, 26-29, Romans 4:13-18, Luke 2:41-52

Reflect:

- Consider the role Joseph had in Jesus' life and what circumstances led to his pivotal role in the story.
- Even though Joseph's role in the story was ordained, it required his faithfulness in standing by Mary's side.
- Consider the obstacles Joseph had to overcome as he stepped up to raise Jesus. What obstacles are you facing and how can you have the faithfulness of Joseph as you face them? What hope can you take from his story?

Respond in Prayer:

✝ It was not through the law that Abraham and his offspring received the promise that he would be heir of the world, but through the righteousness that comes by faith. For if those who depend on the law are heirs, faith means nothing and the promise is worthless, because the law brings wrath. And where there is no law there is no transgression.

Therefore, the promise comes by faith, so that it may be by grace and may be guaranteed to all Abraham's offspring—not only to those who are of the law but also to those who have the faith of Abraham. He is the father of us all. As it is written: "I have made you a father of many nations." He is our father in the sight of God, in whom he believed— the God who gives life to the dead and calls into being things that were not. *(Romans 4:13-17 NIV)*

O God, who from the family of your servant David raised up Joseph to be the guardian of your incarnate Son and the spouse of his virgin mother: Give us grace to imitate his uprightness of life and his obedience to your commands; through Jesus Christ our Lord, who lives and reigns with you and the Holy Spirit, one God, for ever and ever. Amen. *(Collect for the Feast of St. Joseph, BCP)*

Righteousness and justice are the foundations of your throne;
  love and truth go before your face.
Happy are the people who know the festal shout!
  they walk, O Lord, in the light of your presence.
They rejoice daily in your Name;
  they are jubilant in your righteousness.
For you are the glory of their strength,
  and by your favor our might is exalted. *(Psalm 89:14-17 BCP)*

Your love, O Lord, for ever will I sing;
  from age to age my mouth will proclaim your faithfulness.
(Psalm 89:1 BCP)

The Lord's Prayer

"Now then, tell my servant David, 'This is what the Lord Almighty says: I took you from the pasture, from tending the flock, and appointed you ruler over my people Israel. I have been with you wherever you have gone, and I have cut off all your enemies from before you. Now I will make your name great, like the names of the greatest men on earth. And I will provide a place for my people Israel and will plant them so that they can have a home of their own and no longer be disturbed. Wicked people will not oppress them anymore, as they did at the beginning and have done ever since the time I appointed leaders over my people Israel. I will also give you rest from all your enemies. *(2 Samuel 7:8-11 ESV)*

Heavenly Father, I give thanks for your love and your provision. For you see from the beginning to the end and have plans greater than I could ever imagine. You are all-knowing, all-wise, and all-powerful. You have great plans for me, but only as I step forward in faith, trusting in you and placing my hope in you alone. Lord, I want to live a life faithful to you, full of hope in you, and sing your praises to the end. Lead me to be your light in this world. Amen.

Feast of the Annunciation

"I am the Lord's servant," Mary answered. "May your word to me by fulfilled."
(Luke 1:38 NIV)

The Feast of the Annunciation commemorates the Angel Gabriel's visit to Mary to announce her role her as Jesus' mother. It is celebrated on March 25th. It's a celebration of Mary's faithfulness to fulfill the prophecy foretold in Isaiah 7:14 a reminder of the ongoing work of the Holy Spirit in our lives.

Read:
Isaiah 7:10-14, Psalm 40:5-11, Luke 1:26-38

Reflect:
- How do see God's power at work in Mary's story? How he knows the beginning and the end? How he has a bigger pla than you can imagine?
- How might God be at work in your life? What might your r be in his bigger plans?
- How can you open your heart to the work of the Holy Spir in your life? What 'yes' is he waiting for you to give so he c work his glory through your life?

Respond in Prayer:

✠ In the sixth month of Elizabeth's pregnancy, God sent the angel Gabriel to Nazareth, a town in Galilee, to a virgin pledged to be married to a man named Joseph, a descendant of David. The virgin' name was Mary. The angel went to her and said, "Greetings, you w are highly favored! The Lord is with you."

Mary was greatly troubled at his words and wondered what kind of greeting this might be. But the angel said to her, "Do not be afraid, Mary; you have found favor with God. You will conceive and give birth to a son, and you are to call him Jesus. He will be great and w be called the Son of the Most High. The Lord God will give him the throne of his father David, and he will reign over Jacob's descendar forever; his kingdom will never end."

"How will this be," Mary asked the angel, "since I am a virgin?"

The angel answered, "The Holy Spirit will come on you, and the power of the Most High will overshadow you. So the holy one to be born will be called the Son of God. Even Elizabeth your relative is going to have a child in her old age, and she who was said to be unable to conceive is in her sixth month. For no word from God wil ever fail."

"I am the Lord's servant," Mary answered. "May your word to me be fulfilled." Then the angel left her. *(Luke 1:26-38 ESV)*

○ Pour your grace into our hearts, O Lord, that we who have known the incarnation of your Son Jesus Christ, announced by an angel to the Virgin Mary, may by his cross and passion be brought to the glory of his resurrection; who lives and reigns with you, in the unity of the Holy Spirit, one God, now and for ever. Amen. *(Collect for the Feast of the Annunciation, BCP)*

Great things are they that you have done, O Lord my God!
how great your wonders and your plans for us!
there is none who can be compared with you. *(Psalm 40:5 BCP)*

● For nothing will be impossible with God. *(Luke 1:37 NIV)*

○ **The Lord's Prayer**

My soul proclaims the greatness of the Lord,
my spirit rejoices in God my Savior;
    for he has looked with favor on his lowly servant.
From this day all generations will call me blessed:
    the Almighty has done great things for me, and holy is his Name.
He has mercy on those who fear him
    in every generation.
He has shown the strength of his arm,
    he has scattered the proud in their conceit.
He has cast down the mighty from their thrones,
    and has lifted up the lowly.
He has filled the hungry with good things,
    and the rich he has sent away empty.
He has come to the help of his servant Israel,
    for he has remembered his promise of mercy,
The promise he made to our fathers,
    to Abraham and his children for ever.

Glory to the Father, and to the Son, and to the Holy Spirit:
    as it was in the beginning, is now, and will be for ever. Amen.
(Canticle 15 Magnificat, BCP)

Heavenly and almighty Father, your ways are beyond my ways, your thoughts wider and deeper than my own. You know my beginning and my end. You have a role for me in your Kingdom work here on earth. Work in my heart so that I can bring you glory. Lead me to trust in you and be ready to say 'yes' when you call. May I have the faithfulness of Mary to joyfully follow where you lead. Great are you, Lord, and how wonderful are the plans you have for us. There is none who can compare with you. Amen.

Praying for Others

"The prayer of a righteous person is powerful and effective."
(James 5:16 NIV)

Prayer beads are a great way to pray for others. Pray for specific people in your life at each week bead. You can simply pray through your prayer request list or designate each week with a theme to help you identify people to pray over.

For example, you might divide the weeks into prayers for the community, prayers for friends, prayers for family, prayers for you. Or, prayers for the sick, prayers for the grieving, prayers for the struggling, prayers for the poor. Or, prayers for your church leaders, prayers for community leaders, prayers for the government, prayers for those in need.

Whether you choose to pray your own list or use a grouping to guide your prayer, lift up a person or a group of people at each week bead. Pause and pray for their needs, whether known or not.

Pray:

✝ Is anyone among you in trouble? Let them pray. Is anyone happy? Let them sing songs of praise. Is anyone among you sick? Let them call the elders of the church to pray over them and anoint them with oil in the name of the Lord. And the prayer offered in faith will make the sick person well; the Lord will raise them up. If they have sinned, they will be forgiven. Therefore confess your sins to each other and pray for each other so that you may be healed. The prayer of a righteous person is powerful and effective. *(James 5:13-16 NIV)*

◯ Almighty God, who hast promised to hear the petitions of those who ask in thy Son's Name: We beseech thee mercifully to incline thine ear to us who have now made our prayers and supplications unto thee; and grant that those things which we have faithfully asked according to thy will, may effectually be obtained, to the relief of our necessity, and to the setting forth of thy glory; through Jesus Christ our Lord. Amen. *(Collect for the Answer of Prayer, Book of Common Prayer)*

Listen to my words, Lord,
   consider my lament.
Hear my cry for help,
   my King and my God,
   for to you I pray. *(Psalm 5:1-2 NIV)*

Pray for each person on your prayer list today

The Lord's Prayer

But let all who take refuge in you be glad;
   let them ever sing for joy.
Spread your protection over them,
   that those who love your name may rejoice in you.

Surely, Lord, you bless the righteous;
   you surround them with your favor as with a shield.
(Psalm 5:11-12 NIV)

Glory to the Father, and to the Son, and to the Holy Spirit:
   as it was in the beginning, is now, and will be for ever. Amen.
(Canticle 15 Magnificat, BCP)

Praying for Thanksgivings & Blessings

"I will thank you, O LORD my God, with all my heart, and glorify your Name for evermore."
(Psalm 86:12 BCP)

Praying prayers of thanksgivings and blessings is not only a wonderful way to praise God, but also a way to refocus your heart.

When you're feeling anxious, sad, overwhelmed, grieving, or angry, try carving out time to focus on everything good God has done in your life. Spend time taking notice of blessings and give thanks to God for each one.

Prayer beads are a great way to focus on blessings, slowing down your prayers and ensuring you take the time to identify a number of blessings in your life, especially if you're in a season where it's been hard to see them.

You can give each set of Weeks Beads a theme, such as blessings in my family, blessings in my workplace, blessings in my community, blessings in the world. Or, simply pray for a different blessing at each Weeks Bead. Continue going around the circle more than once until you have prayed through all your blessings.

Pray:

Don't fret or worry. Instead of worrying, pray. Let petitions and praises shape your worries into prayers, letting God know your concerns. Before you know it, a sense of God's wholeness, everything coming together for good, will come and settle you down. It's wonderful what happens when Christ displaces worry at the center of your life.

Summing it all up, friends, I'd say you'll do best by filling your minds and meditating on things true, noble, reputable, authentic, compelling, gracious—the best, not the worst; the beautiful, not the ugly; things to praise, not things to curse. Put into practice what you learned from me, what you heard and saw and realized. Do that, and God, who makes everything work together, will work you into his most excellent harmonies. *(Philippians 4:6-8 MSG)*

Accept, O Lord, my thanks and praise for all that you have done for me. I thank you for the splendor of the whole creation, for the beauty of this world, for the wonder of life, and for the mystery of love.

I thank you for the blessing of family and friends, and for the loving care which surrounds me on every side.

I thank you for setting me at tasks which demand my best efforts, and for leading me to accomplishments which satisfy and delight me.

I thank you also for those disappointments and failures that lead me to acknowledge my dependence on you alone.

Above all, I thank you for your Son Jesus Christ; for the truth of his Word and the example of his life; for his steadfast obedience, by which he overcame temptation; for his dying, through which he overcame death; and for his rising to life again, in which I are raised to the life of your kingdom.

Grant me the gift of your Spirit, that I may know him and make him known; and through him, at all times and in all places, may give thanks to you in all things. Amen.

(Prayer for a General Thanksgiving, Book of Common Prayer)

For you are great;
you do wondrous things;
  and you alone are God.

I will thank you, O LORD my God, with all my heart,
  and glorify your Name for evermore. *(Psalm 86:10,12 BCP)*

Give thanks to God for each blessing in your life.

The Lord's Prayer

Rejoice always, pray continually, give thanks in all circumstances; for this is God's will for you in Christ Jesus. (1 Thessalonians 5:16-18 NIV)

Now to him who is able to do far more abundantly than all that we ask or think, according to the power at work within us, 21 to him be glory in the church and in Christ Jesus throughout all generations, forever and ever. Amen. *(Ephesians 3:20-21 ESV)*

Praying for Strength in the Storm

"So do not fear, for I am with you; do not be dismayed, for I am your God."
(Isaiah 41:10 NIV)

When you are surrounded by the storms of life and feel embattled on all sides, t
to God in prayer. Lean on him for strength and support. Release your worries an
issues to him and allow God to carry the burdens. Let God fight for you and find
rest in him.

Pray:

 So do not fear, for I am with you;
    do not be dismayed, for I am your God.
I will strengthen you and help you;
    I will uphold you with my righteous right hand.
"All who rage against you
    will surely be ashamed and disgraced;
those who oppose you
    will be as nothing and perish.
Though you search for your enemies,
    you will not find them.
Those who wage war against you
    will be as nothing at all.
For I am the Lord your God
    who takes hold of your right hand
and says to you, Do not fear;
    I will help you. *(Isaiah 41:10-13 NIV)*

Lord, make us instruments of your peace. Where there is hatred, le
us sow love; where there is injury, pardon; where there is discord,
union; where there is doubt, faith; where there is despair, hope;
where there is darkness, light; where there is sadness, joy. Grant
that we may not so much seek to be consoled as to console; to be
understood as to understand; to be loved as to love. For it is in givi
that we receive; it is in pardoning that we are pardoned; and it is in
dying that we are born to eternal life. Amen. *(A Prayer Attributed to St.
Francis, Book of Common Prayer)*

He gives strength to the weary
    and increases the power of the weak.
Even youths grow tired and weary,
    and young men stumble and fall;
but those who hope in the Lord
    will renew their strength.
They will soar on wings like eagles;
    they will run and not grow weary,
    they will walk and not be faint. *(Isaiah 40:29-31 NIV)*

Come to me, all you who are weary and burdened, and I will give you
rest. *(Matthew 11:28 NIV)*

The Lord's Prayer

The Lord is my light and my salvation—
    whom shall I fear?
The Lord is the stronghold of my life—
    of whom shall I be afraid?

Though an army besiege me,
    my heart will not fear;
though war break out against me,
    even then I will be confident.
(Psalm 27:1,3 NIV)

*Almighty God, your scriptures repeat these words "do not be afraid", yet
I so often am. You say "do not fear", yet fear threatens to overtake me
some days. So, I will place my trust in you, knowing you are by my side
no matter what. You take hold of my right hand and whisper in my ear,
"do not fear, do not be afraid". For I know my help comes from you alone
and you will strengthen me and protect me. Stay by my side and hold my
hand. Amen.*

The Lord gives strength to his people;
    the Lord blesses his people with peace. Amen. *(Psalm 29:11 NIV)*

Praying for Guidance and Direction

When you need guidance or direction on something in your life, seek wisdom from God and allow him to direct your steps. Listening is crucial in your prayers as you seek answers from God. Prayer beads can help you slow down and listen, especially as you pray through God's Word.

Take your time with this prayer, pausing after each bead to listen. As you pray, release your heart and your own plans to God. Allow him to make and mold you, guiding you in his way, in his plans, in his timing. Place your whole trust in God a submit yourself to his guidance.

Pray:

✝ If any of you lacks wisdom, you should ask God, who gives generou to all without finding fault, and it will be given to you. But when yo ask, you must believe and not doubt, because the one who doubts like a wave of the sea, blown and tossed by the wind. *(James 1:5-6 NIV*

○ O God, by whom the meek are guided in judgment, and light rises up in darkness for the godly: Grant us, in all our doubts and uncertainties, the grace to ask what you would have us to do, that the Spirit of wisdom may save us from all false choices, and that in your light we may see light, and in your straight path may not stumble; through Jesus Christ our Lord. Amen. *(Collect for Guidance, Book of Common Prayer)*

Show me your ways, O LORD,
   and teach me your paths.
Lead me in your truth and teach me,
   for you are the God of my salvation;
   in you have I trusted all the day long. *(Psalm 25:3-4 BCP)*

● Your word is a lamp to my feet
   and a light to my path. *(Psalm 119:105 ESV)*

The Lord's Prayer

The Lord will guide you always;
  he will satisfy your needs in a sun-scorched land
  and will strengthen your frame.
You will be like a well-watered garden,
  like a spring whose waters never fail. *(Isaiah 58:11 NIV)*

Trust in the Lord with all your heart
  and lean not on your own understanding;
in all your ways submit to him,
  and he will make your paths straight. *(Proverbs 3:5-6 NIV)*

Now to him who is able to keep you from stumbling and to present you blameless before the presence of his glory with great joy, to the only God, our Savior, through Jesus Christ our Lord, be glory, majesty, dominion, and authority, before all time and now and forever. Amen. *(Jude 1:24-25 ESV)*

Praying for God's Forgiveness

"For your Name's sake, O Lord, forgive my sin, for it is great."
(Psalm 25:10 BCP)

We all sin and err because we are human and broken. Yet, God asks that we confess those sins and turn to him for salvation and reconciliation. We need to acknowledge where we have done wrong and then make a turn in our life to do better.

As you pray this prayer, pause to confess your specific sins and ask God for forgiveness. Consider how what changes you need to make in order to fully repent and commit those to God. Ask for his help in making these changes to more closely follow in his way.

Pray:

Have mercy on me, O God,
    according to your steadfast love;
according to your abundant mercy
    blot out my transgressions.
Wash me thoroughly from my iniquity,
    and cleanse me from my sin.

For I know my transgressions,
    and my sin is ever before me.
Against you, you alone, have I sinned,
    and done what is evil in your sight,
so that you are justified in your sentence
    and blameless when you pass judgment.
Indeed, I was born guilty,
    a sinner when my mother conceived me.

You desire truth in the inward being;
    therefore teach me wisdom in my secret heart.
Purge me with hyssop, and I shall be clean;
    wash me, and I shall be whiter than snow.
Let me hear joy and gladness;
    let the bones that you have crushed rejoice.
Hide your face from my sins,
    and blot out all my iniquities.

Create in me a clean heart, O God,
    and put a new and right spirit within me. *(Psalm 51:1-10 NRSV)*

○ I confess to Almighty God, to his Church, and to you, that I have sinned by my own fault in thought, word, and deed, in things done and left undone; especially _____. For these and all other sins which I cannot now remember, I am truly sorry. I pray God to have mercy on me. I firmly intend amendment of life, and I humbly beg forgiveness of God and his Church, and ask you for counsel, direction, and absolution. *(Prayer for the Reconciliation of a Penitent, Book of Common Prayer)*

Remember, O LORD, your compassion and love,
    for they are from everlasting.
Remember not the sins of my youth and my transgressions;
    remember me according to your love
    and for the sake of your goodness, O LORD. *(Psalm 25:5-6 BCP)*

● For your Name's sake, O LORD,
    forgive my sin, for it is great. *(Psalm 25:10 BCP)*

(As you pray at each Weeks Bead, you can pause to pray through specifics of the sins you are confessing or how you will repent and make changes. Or simply pray these verses, allowing God's forgiveness and mercy to wash over you.)

○ *The Lord's Prayer*

✝ As for you, you were dead in your transgressions and sins, in which you used to live when you followed the ways of this world and of the ruler of the kingdom of the air, the spirit who is now at work in those who are disobedient. All of us also lived among them at one time, gratifying the cravings of our flesh and following its desires and thoughts. Like the rest, we were by nature deserving of wrath. But because of his great love for us, God, who is rich in mercy, made us alive with Christ even when we were dead in transgressions—it is by grace you have been saved. And God raised us up with Christ and seated us with him in the heavenly realms in Christ Jesus, in order that in the coming ages he might show the incomparable riches of his grace, expressed in his kindness to us in Christ Jesus. For it is by grace you have been saved, through faith—and this is not from yourselves, it is the gift of God— not by works, so that no one can boast. For we are God's handiwork, created in Christ Jesus to do good works, which God prepared in advance for us to do. *(Ephesians 2:1-10 NIV)*

Now may our Lord Jesus Christ himself and God our Father, who loved us and through grace gave us eternal comfort and good hope, comfort your hearts and strengthen them in every good work and word. Amen. *(2 Thessalonians 2:16-17 NRSV)*

Made in the USA
Coppell, TX
25 January 2023